SOUND DOCTRINE

Teaching that leads to true fear of the Lord

by Torben Søndergaard

SOUND DOCTRINE

Teaching that leads to true fear of the Lord

TORBEN SØNDERGAARD

SOUND DOCTRINE
Teaching that leads to true fear of the Lord

By Torben Søndergaard

Paperback: ISBN: 978-1-938526-45-9

ePub (iBooks, Nook): ISBN: 978-1-938526-46-6

Mobi (Kindle): ISBN: 978-1-938526-47-3

eBook: ISBN: 978-1-938526-53-4

Published by LAURUS BOOKS

LAURUS BOOKS
P. O. Box 894
Locust Grove, GA 30248 USA
www.LaurusBooks.com

This book may be purchased in paperback from TheLaurusCompany.com, Amazon.com, and other retailers around the world. Also available in formats for electronic readers from their respective stores.

TABLE OF CONTENTS

PREFACE

It is a great joy to be able to present *Sound Doctrine* in English. This is a different and prophetic book that has not been written on the basis of a good idea, but out of a call from God. At the beginning of 2001, God gave me the message of *Sound Doctrine* one chapter at a time each day for almost two weeks.

After that, I waiting for God to tell me when it was time to publish the book, or if it was even to be published. He did that almost three years after I had completed the writing and, at the same time, told me to write a preface telling how it came into existence and a postscript titled "Three Years Later."

Sound Doctrine is not just a book with a message. It is also a testimony of how the true Word of God has changed my life. I am sure it will change the lives of many others when they receive this message.

The book is divided in the following way:

- First, this preface that contains the testimony of how *Sound Doctrine* came into existence and how, since that time, God has confirmed His Word in my life.
- Next in line is the book itself, *Sound Doctrine*, as I got it chapter by chapter in the year 2001.
- Finally, a postscript where I sum up and deepen the message and go into more detail about *Sound Doctrine* according to what God has shown me.

Longing to bear fruit

At the end of the year 2000, I began to look at my life and to consider its fruits. I have had a longing to serve God since I got saved in 1995. Since then, I have done many things to reach people. Most people in the surrounding churches knew me as a bold young man who was on fire for God and very active. Although I was very bold, witnessed to many people about Christ, and was known for that in the churches, I discovered that I had almost no lasting fruit from what I did. I could not think of one person who had truly come to God through what I did, or who had been healed or set free from demons. Together with others, I had probably prayed for one or two who were healed, but that was it. The more I thought about this, the more dissatisfied I became with my life's fruit. I was not satisfied with the fact that the Christians thought I was doing a lot when there were no visible results to find.

One day while I was thinking about this, I read a parable in the Bible that led to the beginning of a transformation in my life.

> *Then Jesus used this illustration: "A man planted a fig tree in his garden and came again and again to see if there was any fruit on it, but he was always disappointed. Finally, he said to his gardener, 'I've waited three years, and there hasn't been a single fig! Cut it down. It's taking up space we can use for something else.' The gardener answered, 'Give it one more chance. Leave it another year, and I'll give it special attention and plenty of fertilizer. If we get figs next year, fine. If not, you can cut it down.'"* (Luke 13:6-9 NLT)

When I read this parable, I experienced God speaking to me. I felt that I was like this fig tree that did not bear fruit. The difference between the tree and me was that I had been without fruit not just for three years, but five.

When I realized this, I understood that something had to happen immediately! I could not continue like that. If I did not start to bear fruit, then I would be cut down, just as it was written in the parable about the fig tree. I said to God: "Okay, give me one year, and if I then do not bear fruit, take my life and cut me down, for then nothing matters anymore." Maybe this sounds a bit too radical, but I had seen that God demands fruit in our lives, and there were no excuses.

40 days of fasting

I decided overnight that I would fast for forty days and seek God. I had to start bearing fruit in my life, as God demands. My fast began on January 3, 2001. I began by drinking only water, but, later, I drank some juice and a little cocoa to get some quick energy, even though it is not the exact right way to do it. In this period of fasting, I really experienced how God's Word came alive to me. I did not pray much more than I usually did, but I read and studied the Word of God. One Scripture after another came alive to me, as if it was something new that God had just written.

After the forty days of fasting, I was filled up with new revelations from God, and I was filled with the Word as never before. I thought of the Word of God and meditated on it day and night, including while I was sleeping. It was a really special experience.

Shortly after that, I felt that I had to express some of the things God had given me, so I sat down by my computer and started to write. When I had written five or six pages, size A4 (8.3 x 11.7 inches), I stopped and thought, "What am I going to use this for?" There was too much content for my website (oplevjesus.dk), and it did not fit the purpose of the website either, which was aimed at reaching non-Christians. This teaching was for Christians. Therefore, I did not know what to do with the things I had written.

While I was thinking about all this, God spoke to me. I will never forget it. It was so clear. He said three words to me: "Write a book!" I stopped, looked up, and said, "WHAT? Write a book? Do you really mean that? Have you forgotten that my lowest grades were in writing and spelling when I finished school?" That was one year before I wrote the booklet, "Deceived," which has now been printed in several editions. At that time, I was not used to writing long texts.

God did not answer my objections but spoke again and said just as clearly as before: "You shall write a book, and I will give you one chapter each day. But on Sundays, you shall not write. You shall have time off together with your family."

"Wow," I thought, "I'm going to write a book." That was an incredible experience that I will never forget.

I know that some of you have become arrogant, thinking I will never visit you again. But I will come—and soon—if the Lord will let me, and then I'll find out whether these arrogant people are just big talkers or whether they really have God's power. For the Kingdom of God is not just fancy talk; it is living by God's power. Which do you choose? Should I come with punishment and scolding, or should I come with quiet love and gentleness? (1 Corinthians 4:18-21 NLT)

"Wow, how big." I was totally excited. I knew it was from God, and I looked forward to experiencing it. The interesting thing was that, at that time, I had not seen anyone whom I had prayed for getting healed, and there was no lasting fruit in my life.

God Confirms His Word

Since the day that God spoke this, I knew that something would happen, and so it did. It was not even one week before I prayed for three people who got healed. I experienced very strongly how God let me get started with the things He had for me. After one good week, I was at home relaxing, and then it came to me: "Now something will happen." In the same minute, I received a phone call. It was someone from the church who asked if I wanted to go with him and talk to the people on the street. I said: "Yes, I would like to do that," because God had just told me that something would happen. The guy who had called came and picked me up, and we went downtown.

When we were about to park the car, I saw a girl walking with crutches together with her mother. I knew right away that God would heal her. I jumped out of the car, ran toward her, told her that I was a Christian, and asked if I could pray for her. She allowed me to do so. I put my hand on her foot, which was sprained, prayed a short prayer, and told her that she should try to walk. She did not dare at first, so I told her not to be afraid because she was healed. Then she slowly tried to use her foot. She quickly realized that it was true and that she had really been healed. I talked to them a little longer, and, when they were about to go, the girl walked normally while her mother carried the crutches.

Since then, I have experienced many things. In one year, I prayed for about 150 people who got healed, and ten of them threw away their crutches. I have also seen many more people receive the Lord Jesus

Christ and really surrender themselves to Him and, today, are living strong with God. They are people I met downtown, in the supermarket, the library, and so on. At that time, I was not a speaker, so it all happened outside the meetings or the church.

When God said that I should wait to publish this book until He told me to do so, I thought it would take a few months, or perhaps half a year, but that was not the case. Finally, after three years, the time came.

God did many things during those three years. I have experienced many people getting their life changed by God's power. I have seen many give their life to God and are truly living for Him still today.

About a year after all this started, I published a booklet that I felt I should write called "Deceived?" It is now out in its second edition, about 10,000 copies, and many of them are already sold. At least seven people I know personally got saved just by reading this booklet and are living close to God today. I have also heard of many others around the country who got saved or met God through the booklet.

I have been on the radio and TV many times, and people have been healed by watching. Some of those whom God has healed through me have told about it on TV.

On October 16, 2002, I was on a show called "19-Direct" on Denmark's biggest TV channel, DR. We talked about God and healing. As the show was coming to an end, I was allowed to pray for the viewers through the TV. The result was that many people around the country got healed in their living rooms in front of their TV sets. Because of those healings, they talked about them the next day during the same show, and they had an interview with one person who got healed through the TV. It was a lady who, for many years, had not been able to lift her arm because of a frozen shoulder. When I prayed for the sick through the TV, she got healed and could lift her arm without any problems. Since then, I have met many around the country who have said they, or someone they knew, got healed through that prayer.

On October 29, 2003, God opened the door into DR's "19-Direct" for me again. This time, they showed how I prayed for a young man in "Jesus Shop" (a Christian bookshop) in Herning who got healed. One of his legs had been in a plaster cast because he had partly broken off one of the bones in his foot two days earlier. I cut the plaster cast and broke it off his leg because he had been healed. The last thing they showed on TV was him leaving the shop without the plaster cast, sock, and shoe. He was supposed to wear the plaster cast for one week and then have another kind of plaster cast put on his foot for about eight weeks. He went home healed, with both crutches in one hand. When this was shown on TV, I personally received a lot of responses from people all over the country who wanted to be prayed for. Many have been healed and have met Jesus since then through this broadcast.

There is much more to say about what God has done. He has really confirmed His Word in my life, as He said He would. Because of that, if people go against this book, I can ask: "What about the power?" The Kingdom of God is not just fancy talk; it is living by God's power.

Please understand that I am not saying this because of pride. I really fear God and know that I am totally dependent on Him because I can do nothing by myself. I am saying this with fear and trembling. I just want to get His Word out, and I want us, His people, to come back to sound doctrine. There is still much more to see, and I have only seen a small portion of it. God has so much for all of us to take hold of. However, I am writing about my experience so that you can understand that God is powerful, and that He really wants us, His people, to come back to His Word as it is.

I know that I have received a message from God that I am to preach, and what I am sharing in this book is only a small part of it. However, I believe that it will open up new doors for His Word. Since I wrote *Sound Doctrine,* I have seen and understood much more. It started here, and even though I wanted to go deeper in some areas, I knew that I should not rewrite the chapters.

Now the time came

After three years of wondering if I would ever publish this book, God spoke to me on October 4, 2003, and said that the time had come. It was very special. I prayed and did not feel anything, but suddenly, God spoke and said that now was the time for me to publish *Sound Doctrine*. He told me to add a preface to tell how the book came about and a postscript to sum up and go deeper into some parts of the book.

God also spoke to me about another book I should write. At first,

I thought the messages in the new book should be published as a teaching on a CD, but He wanted them to be published in a book connected with *Sound Doctrine*. That book would be titled *Life of a Christian* and would consist of three messages: "Christians and Sin," "Christians and Faith," and "Christians and the Supernatural." It would be a teaching about what faith and sin are, what they mean to us, and how the supernatural should be a natural part of being a Christian.

As I have proceeded, I have realized the importance of the teaching. Through that, God has revealed many things to me and those I have been teaching. It has already been a great blessing, and I am really looking forward to publishing the book.

We are in great need of sound teaching. Much of what we have been taught pleases people instead of being the true Word of God, the doctrine that brings true and sound fear of the Lord.

As a beginning, you can now read *Sound Doctrine* as God gave it to me. I know that I experienced something that God has for everyone. Receive the message, and let Him come in and transform your life. We have to return to the essentials. Solomon ends the book of Ecclesiastes by saying:

> *But, my child, be warned: There is no end of opinions ready to be expressed. Studying them can go on forever and become very exhausting! Here is my final conclusion: Fear God and obey his commands, for this is the duty of every person. God will judge us for everything we do, including every secret thing, whether good or bad.* (Ecclesiastes 12:12-14 NLT)

Enjoy the reading of *Sound Doctrine*, and may God bless you through this message.

—Torben Søndergaard

INTRODUCTION

If we look at churches today, both Lutheran and evangelical churches, we see that sin is not spoken of much. When we come from an evangelical church and tell someone how to become a Christian, we can do it almost without saying what the problem really is: namely, sin that separates us from God. We might mention a few Scriptures about how we all have sinned and come short of the glory of God and that we need Jesus. This is almost everything that is said about sin. Then we mention, for example, Romans 10:9-10, that if you confess with your mouth and believe in your heart that God has raised Him from the dead, you shall be saved. We pray a prayer and let the person repeat it, and then: "Congratulations, you are a new creation. You are on your way to heaven. Now, remember to pray to God, read your Bible, and go to church."

In some denominations, you do not even have to open your mouth to get "saved." You just have to get a little water sprinkled on your head, and then you belong to the Kingdom of God. Of course, this is not how it is done everywhere, but people are mostly introduced to the gospel without mentioning sin. If it is mentioned, then most often it is not about repenting from the sinful way of living, which means specific sins, but turning away to a new life where you can do almost the same things you did before. The difference is "just" that you are on your way to heaven.

The situation today is that, in many cases, we cannot determine if people are Christians by looking at their lifestyles. The immediate visible difference might be that the Christian is a little more kind, does not curse, and, of course, goes to church on Sunday. Actually, "Christians" can do almost the same things as non-Christians. We can drink alcohol, as long as we don't get drunk. We can watch the same movies. We can spend our time on the same things that people in the world do. Yes, we are almost like "the world." You might say, "But we have to be friends with people or else we can't reach them. Jesus spent time with sinners." It is true that Jesus spent time with sinners, but the difference between Him and many Christians today is that He did not compromise with sin in any way. It was not the sinners who influenced Him; He influenced the sinners. He spent time with them, but He was not a friend of "the world" (James 4:4).

I pray that everyone who reads this book will have their eyes opened to see the truth in God's Word, so that we do not continue to be deceived by this world and its god, "the Devil." God has a plan for each Christian and each church in this country, but I do not believe we will get the breakthrough we long for unless our relationship to sin is changed—in each of our lives individually and in the church of God in general.

What comes first, sanctification or revival?

1

GOD IS HOLY

Obey God because you are his children. Don't slip back into your old ways of doing evil; you didn't know any better then. But now you must be holy in everything you do, just as God—who chose you to be his children—is holy. For he himself has said, "You must be holy because I am holy." (1 Peter 1:14-16 NLT)

God is holy and He cannot have fellowship with sin. That was why He had to sacrifice Jesus in order to cleanse us from sin so that He could have fellowship with us again. It is important for us as Christians that we do not continue to live in sin, but that we let God change us. If we still live in sin, we shall die.

So put to death the sinful, earthly things lurking within you. Have nothing to do with sexual sin, impurity, lust, and shameful desires. Don't be greedy for the good things of this life, for that is idolatry. God's terrible anger will come upon those who do such things. You used to do them when your life was still part of this world. But now is the time to get rid of anger, rage, malicious behavior, slander, and dirty language. Don't lie to each other, for you have stripped off your old evil nature and all its wicked deeds. In its place you have clothed yourselves with a brand-new nature that is continually being renewed as you learn more and more about Christ, who created this new nature within you. (Colossians 3:5-10 NLT)

Our life as a Christian is a walk, a walk toward eternal life and the crown of righteousness that God will give to those who win. However, it is so important that we do not give up, or else we will miss the reward. Unfortunately, there are many people who once lived with God, but do not live with Him today. They had fellowship with Him, but now they will end up in eternal perdition. Make a decision now to reach the goal. Decide today that you are not going to lose the treasure that God has given you. Stretch out to get it. Reach for the goal, as Paul says:

No, dear brothers and sisters, I am still not all I should be, but I am focusing all my energies on this one thing: Forgetting the past and looking forward to what lies ahead, I strain to reach the end of the race and receive the prize for which God, through Christ Jesus, is calling us up to heaven. (Philippians 3:13-14 NLT)

Let God come. Open up your life to Him so He can change you. Choose today whom you want to serve—sin, which ends with eternal perdition (hell), or God, which ends with eternal life (Romans 6:20).

2

Basics of Christianity

So let us stop going over the basics of Christianity again and again. Let us go on instead and become mature in our understanding. Surely we don't need to start all over again with the importance of turning away from evil deeds and placing our faith in God. You don't need further instruction about baptisms, the laying on of hands, the resurrection of the dead, and eternal judgment. And so, God willing, we will move forward to further understanding. For it is impossible to restore to repentance those who were once enlightened—those who have experienced the good things of heaven and shared in the Holy Spirit, who have tasted the goodness of the word of God and the power of the age to come—and who then turn away from God. It is impossible to bring such people to repentance again because they are nailing the Son of God to the cross again by rejecting him, holding him up to public shame. (Hebrews 6:1-6 NLT)

We read here in Hebrews 6:1 that the basics of Christianity for believers are "turning away (repenting) from evil deeds." The most fundamental thing when becoming and being a Christian is repentance and faith. Sin was the reason why Jesus had to die for us.

When Adam sinned, sin entered the entire human race. Adam's sin brought death, so death spread to everyone, for everyone sinned. (Romans 5:12 NLT)

Jesus came with the message of repentance, and He passed it on to us that we should go into the world and cause people to repent. Some may argue, "No, that is not true. Jesus came with the message that we should believe in Him, and that everyone who believes in Him shall not perish, but have eternal life." Yes, that is also true, but believing and repenting work together.

Repentance

At the beginning of the gospel of Matthew, we see that John the Baptist came with this message:

"Repent, for the kingdom of heaven is at hand." (Matthew 3:2 NASB)

He came with the message of repentance. You might say, "Well, that was John, and that was before Jesus started to preach." Let's look at Jesus then. In Matthew 4, we see that Jesus was in the desert for 40 days and nights where He was tempted by the Devil. After 40 days, He began to preach. Let's see what He said:

From that time Jesus began to preach and say, "Repent, for the kingdom of heaven is at hand." (Matthew 4:17 NASB)

In the gospel of Mark, Jesus said that the Kingdom of God is near and they should repent and believe (have faith) in the gospel (Mark 1:15). Here we see that He first talked about repentance and then about faith. It is not quite the same as we hear in the churches today. Jesus said:

"I have come to call sinners to turn from their sins, not to spend my time with those who think they are already good enough." (Luke 5:32 NLT)

In Luke 15, we can read the story of the lost sheep and that Jesus leaves the ninety-nine other sheep to go and look for the lost one. At the end, we read:

Thus, I tell you, there will be more joy in heaven over one [especially] wicked person who repents (changes his mind, abhorring his errors and misdeeds, and determines to enter upon a better course of life) than over ninety-nine righteous persons who have no need of repentance. (Luke 15:7 AMP)

Therefore, there will be more joy over one sinner who *believes* than over ninety-nine righteous ones who do not ... NO, that is not what it says. There is more joy over one sinner who *repents*. Obviously, faith also has to be there because, without faith, it is impossible to please God (Hebrews 11:6). However, faith is expressed through our deeds and repentance (James 2:14-26). Peter explains the message of repentance very well here:

> *So then, since Christ suffered physical pain, you must arm yourselves with the same attitude he had, and be ready to suffer, too. For if you are willing to suffer for Christ, you have decided to stop sinning. And you won't spend the rest of your life chasing after evil desires, but you will be anxious to do the will of God. You have had enough in the past of the evil things that godless people enjoy—their immorality and lust, their feasting and drunkenness and wild parties, and their terrible worship of idols. Of course, your former friends are very surprised when you no longer join them in the wicked things they do, and they say evil things about you. But just remember that they will have to face God, who will judge everyone, both the living and the dead.* (1 Peter 4:1-5 NLT)

Therefore, to repent is to go from following human lusts to following God's will and no longer living a life of immorality, lust, wild parties, and other things, as we did before we repented. This repentance will make others wonder, and they will see that something has happened in our life. Both John the Baptist and Jesus came with the message of repentance. Then what about us?

> *... and that repentance for forgiveness of sins would be proclaimed in His name to all the nations, beginning from Jerusalem.* (Luke 24:47 NASB)

> *And Peter answered them, Repent (change your views and purpose to accept the will of God in your inner selves instead of rejecting it) and be baptized, every one of you, in the name of Jesus Christ for the forgiveness of and release from your sins; and you shall receive the gift of the Holy Spirit.* (Acts 2:38 AMP)

The message at the time of Jesus and today is repentance in the name of Jesus for the forgiveness of sins. Let's ask ourselves if there is something here today that we as churches have lost. We often hear in our churches today: *"Anyone who calls on the name of the Lord will be saved"* (Romans 10:13 NLT), but we rarely hear: *"... 'Those who claim to belong to the Lord must turn away from all wickedness'"* (2 Timothy 2:19 NLT). Both Scriptures are equally true.

Come to Jesus

When I came to faith in Jesus Christ in 1995, I heard nothing from the speaker about repenting from the sin in my old life. I just said: "Jesus, I believe that you died for me. Come and be Lord of my life," and so on, and that was it. I was born again. At that time, I did not know that it was sin that separated me from God and that I should not continue to live the way I did before.

Of course, something happened. I became a new creation, and, in time, I began to repent for my old life. I held on to God. By His grace, I had a strong meeting with Him when I gave my life to Jesus, which made me willing to lay down everything because I knew that what I had experienced was right. I have not left God at any time since then. I have had hard times, but I did not go back into "the world" where I came from.

Unfortunately, that is not what we see in many cases today. If all the people who say yes to Jesus in the streets or in the church held on to Him, then things would look different. I think one of the reasons is that we give them a gospel that is way too cheap, and, in some ways, false as well. We make everything sound so good and so sweet. "Come to Jesus, and you will be much happier. Come to Jesus, and you will receive everything you ask for. Come to Jesus ..." and so on. And people say yes. Why? Well, it sounds pretty good. However, when they are told afterward that they cannot continue to do the things they did before, and they find out that believing in God is not always so much fun, when they experience opposition and troubles, which will always come, then they backslide. Why? Can it be that they were not ready to lay down their old life and truly give their life to Jesus? If someone is born too quickly and in a wrong position, then it might end with a miscarriage.

If we face people who are in control of their lives and feel happy, we sometimes think that we have nothing to offer them. Once, I spoke to a Christian friend who had a non-Christian friend, but he did not think there was any reason to tell him about Jesus because he was all right. He had a good family, a good job, and so on. He had spoken to him about Jesus once, though, but his friend did not feel that he needed Him because he had a great life, which my Christian friend then agreed with. It is scary to hear something like this, but, unfortunately, it happens in many places. We forget that they are sinners on their way to hell. I think one of the reasons why we do not see as many "successful" people saved as we see, for example, drug addicts is that we do not preach the true gospel. No matter how much money people have and how great their life is right now, they are still sinners on their way to hell. They need to know that they are sinners. People cannot repent and receive salvation until they see themselves as sinners. That is one of the reasons why we have the Law:

For no person will be justified (made righteous, acquitted, and judged acceptable) in His sight by observing the works prescribed by the Law. For [the real function of] the Law is to make men recognize and be conscious of sin [not mere perception, but an acquaintance with sin which works toward repentance, faith, and holy character]. (Romans 3:20 AMP)

The Ten Commandments

Once a religious leader asked Jesus this question: "Good teacher, what should I do to get eternal life?" "Why do you call me good?" Jesus asked him. "Only God is truly good. But as for your question, you know the commandments: 'Do not commit adultery. Do not murder. Do not steal. Do not testify falsely. Honor your father and mother.'" The man replied, "I've obeyed all these commandments since I was a child." "There is still one thing you lack," Jesus said. "Sell all you have and give the money to the poor, and you will have treasure in heaven. Then come, follow me." But when the man heard this, he became sad because he was very rich. (Luke 18:18-23 NLT)

Here we see a person who comes and asks Jesus: *"What should I do to receive eternal life?"* Today, we would say that you have to believe in Jesus with all your heart and confess it with your mouth.

Here, however, Jesus talks about the Law, the Ten Commandments. Why does He mention the Ten Commandments? The rich man needed to see himself as a sinner. You cannot repent and receive forgiveness if you cannot see yourself as a sinner.

I once read an autobiography of Charles Finney, one of the world's greatest evangelists. He came to speak in a town where one of the members of the local church council was not a born-again Christian.

His wife, who *was* born-again, could not understand why her husband could not or did not want to receive Jesus. When she later spoke to Charles Finney, they came to the conclusion that her husband's big issue was that he was so nice and kind and lived such a good and right life that he was righteous in his own eyes. This self-righteousness hindered him from getting saved. Charles Finney and this man's wife prayed to God to remove the self-righteousness, so he could see himself as a sinner. The following day when this man woke up, his self-righteousness was gone, and, for the first time, he saw himself as a sinner and was able to receive forgiveness. He repented, and Jesus became Lord of his life.

One of the problems we have today is that we do not give people the true gospel about repentance and faith in Jesus as Lord and Redeemer. We don't share the message that we have to die to our old life and live a whole new and holy life so that we do not perish forever into the fire of hell. Charles Finney talked about repentance. He spoke God's Word as it is. Of all the thousands of people he led to Jesus, there were only a few who did not reach the goal. Of course, it was not that he just spoke the Word, but he also lived a life in repentance, holiness, and prayer. He experienced that:

> *For the word of God is living and active. Sharper than any double-edged sword, it penetrates even to dividing soul and spirit, joints and marrow; it judges the thoughts and attitudes of the heart."* (Hebrews 4:12 NIV)

We can learn much by looking at Charles Finney's life.

Let us ask ourselves these questions: Do we experience God's Word as a sword? Does God confirm His Word to us by signs and wonders? (Acts 14:3).

There are probably several reasons why we do not experience this very often. For example, lack of holiness and prayer. Can one of the reasons also be that we do not fully preach the Word of God? Let us be willing to lay down everything we have been taught until now and investigate if it is in accordance with God's Word.

"Test everything. Hold on to the good." (1 Thessalonians 5:21 NIV)

3

THE SOUND DOCTRINE

Preach the Word; be prepared in season and out of season; correct, rebuke and encourage—with great patience and careful instruction. For the time will come when men will not put up with sound doctrine. Instead, to suit their own desires, they will gather around them a great number of teachers to say what their itching ears want to hear. They will turn their ears away from the truth and turn aside to myths. But you, keep your head in all situations... (2 Timothy 4:2-5 NIV)

Verses two and three say: "*The time will come when men will not put up with sound doctrine. Instead, to suit their own desires, they will gather around them a great number of teachers to say what their itching ears want to hear. They will turn their ears away from the truth and turn aside to myths.*" The time to which the Bible is referring is now. We see it in our churches today.

In many denominations in the world today, they teach that when you get baptized as a child, then you belong to the Kingdom of God and everything is fine. That is a lie directly from hell. I know people raised in a Christian family who did not dare to drive for a long trip with their little child before he or she was baptized. What if something happened? Today, many baptisms are held in hospitals. If you have a sick baby, or one is born prematurely, and you do not know if the baby will survive, you can call upon a priest to come and baptize the baby.

What deception we are living in! If a little water on a baby's head makes the difference, then it is the parents who are making the decision. It your parents decide, then it is not up to you if you want to believe and get saved, is it? No way. I was both baptized and confirmed as a child, but I would still have perished if I had died before April 1995. Why? Because I was not in Christ. I lived my "own" life in sin, without fellowship with Jesus.

Most of us can see that what is happening in some churches is a deception. At the baby baptism, you are told that everything is all right now. And after a long life, when the child dies without God, the priest says at the funeral that he belonged to God's Kingdom through the baptism, but that is a deception.

Unfortunately, the 82% of Denmark's population who are members of the Lutheran church are not all on their way to Heaven. What is the situation like in some evangelical churches? Are things going any better there? What does the Word of God say? Is everything all right when you are baptized as an adult? Are you "once saved, always saved"? Can you perish when you are baptized with the Holy Spirit and speak in tongues? Do we preach the Word of God, or is it a mixture of humanism and Christianity? Do we only preach the things people want to hear?

"But God is love." Yes, but do you not show love by telling the truth so people can be set free? I have one specific Scripture in mind that says: *"... not many of you should become teachers in the church, for we who teach will be judged by God with greater strictness"* (James 3:1 NLT).

Why will they be judged with greater strictness? It is because they are responsible for preaching the true Word of God. It is so important that we do not hold back the truth.

Much of the teaching I am writing here is very different from what we hear in the churches today. I know that the Scripture quoted above is also valid for me. That is why it is important to be able to confirm everything from God's Word. Many use a Scripture and have teachings based upon it, even if the Scripture is totally out of context and has a completely different meaning. I will show you some examples later on. We must remember that:

The sum of Your word is truth ... (Psalm 119:160 NASB)

I began to think about a study made in November 2000 in ninety-two state churches in Copenhagen that showed how preaching was done. That Sunday, all of the priests were to speak about Matthew 18:1-14, a text that clearly states there are only two ways out after this life: heaven or hell. The majority of the priests treated the subject vaguely, with only about one out of ten churches even mentioning the subject. For example, there were two places where the priests adamantly objected to the message about eternal perdition. One said that verses 6 through 11 did not belong in the Bible because that was not a loving speech. Another one used the parable about the lost sheep as proof that there is no such thing as perdition. Apart from those, there were many other examples of the text being misinterpreted. Read again:

For the time will come when people will not put up with sound doctrine. Instead, to suit their own desires, they will gather around them a great number of teachers to say what their itching ears want to hear. They will turn their ears away from the truth and turn aside to myths. (2 Timothy 4:3-4 NIV)

We are living in this time right now, but let us not just look at others. Let us look at our own lives and our churches.

Conforms to Godliness

In 2 Timothy 4:3, we are told that men will not put up with sound doctrine. But what is "sound doctrine"?

If anyone advocates a different doctrine and does not agree with sound words, those of our Lord Jesus Christ, and with the doctrine conforming to godliness, he is conceited and understands nothing..." (1 Timothy 6:3-4 NASB)

Therefore, the Bible tells us that sound doctrine conforms to godliness.

Paul, a servant of God and an apostle of Jesus Christ to further the faith of God's elect and the knowledge of the truth that leads to godliness ... (Titus 1:1 NIV)

The time will come when men will not put up with sound doctrine that leads to the fear of the Lord.

Proverbs 1:7 (NIV) says: *"The fear of the LORD is the beginning of knowledge …"* I believe this is the right place to begin.

The words "fear of the Lord" have just recently been revealed to me. In my first four or five years as a Christian, I went to many services and heard many sermons, but I never heard these words. It was either because I did not listen well enough or because they are rarely mentioned in the churches today. I do not think there is anything wrong with my ears. Fear of the Lord is something rarely spoken of today. If it is even mentioned, then it is most likely given a different meaning than its original intent.

Before we move on, I would like to share a testimony from my own life. I have experienced that God has been working in my life. I feel that my life has been under His sharp light, and all sin has come out. I have experienced a new dimension of God, a Holy God Who cannot have fellowship with sin.

"… God is light; in him there is no darkness at all." (1 John 1:5 NIV)

I have received the fear of the Lord, which I had never known before, and that made me begin to live a more holy and pure life. I dealt with the sin I had struggled with before, and I experience that, perhaps for the first time, I am really free from sin. Today, I do not feel bound by sin.

Not sinning

The Bible tells us that we should hate what is evil (Romans 12:9), and that has truly become real for me. I hate sin. I can still do something that I later find out to be wrong, and God is still working on my stability, revealing new things that I should stop doing. However, today, I do not fall into the same sin again and again. I used to watch something on TV that was not good, and I would repent, but a little time afterward, I fell into the same sin again. It is not like that anymore. Today, I know that if I live in sin, I can lose my salvation. This sounds radical, and you will probably give me a lot of Scriptures to prove that this is unbiblical. Maybe you are saying: "God is not like that. He is good, and what you are saying is not from Him." I understand you, but the striking part is that after I had received this fear of the Lord, I experienced a total victory. Thanks to that, I do not dare or want to do anything I know is wrong.

When you hear this, it might sound like living in fear, which can stop one from lifting a finger in fear of doing something wrong. At first, it might seem right to believe that, but the truth is absolutely different. I feel more free than ever before in relation to sin. Read Romans 6. I have greater boldness toward God (1 John 3:21). I have dealt with sin that used to bind me. And the best thing of all is that I have become so utterly dependent on Jesus. I know that I cannot make it without Him. I have become so grateful for what He has done for me, and that has made me pray and read my Bible more than ever before.

I have experienced that God has opened my eyes, so that I see many things in a different way. That is one of the reasons why I dare to write a book like this. I know that it will meet opposition because, in many ways, it defies much of what many people stand for and believe in today. I have, therefore, studied the Bible as never before to know if this book is really in accordance with God's Word. Through this, I have experienced indescribable freedom in relation to God and to sin. My prayer is that the readers of this book may experience the same freedom. I pray that it may create true fear of the Lord in your life. It is important to understand that the fear of the Lord is very different from the form of fear that the world brings that binds us even more.

… God is love … There is no fear in love … (1 John 4:16,18 NIV)

The fear of the Lord that I have experienced is not the same fear the world gives. Fear of the Lord sets us free. I pray that, through His Word, God may lead us into what He has for us as individuals and as His church so we can come to the right place and see our country, wherever we live, changed, as we believe and pray for.

Before we move on

Before we move on with the teaching, is it really important that you understand the difference between living in sin and happening to do something wrong—finding out later that what you did was not so good— or falling into sin. When I am telling you that I have gained power over sin, it does not mean that I am never going to do anything wrong. I am still being brought up by God, and He is calling me into a higher level of purity and holiness all the time. There are, for example, things I did just two years ago (before the time of this writing) that I do not do now because God has revealed to me that they are wrong. If I do the same things today, then I commit sin willfully. Before it was revealed to me as sin, it was not conscious sin, or willful sin (John 15:22).

The Bible also tells us about some specific sins, such as fornication, murder, lies, hatred, envy, and adultery, etc. Everybody knows these things are sin because our conscience testifies that they are sin. If you practice these sins anyway, there is no excuse for it (Romans 2:14-15). You can go so far into sin that your conscience is seared, and you will not see sin as sin anymore, or you will not let God speak to you about anything wrong. This does not mean that you will start to do the right thing. If you close your eyes to God's upbringing, it will end badly. The important thing is that we let God come through to us with His Word, so that our mind and judgment are being renewed all the time, so we can discern what God's will is and distinguish between right and wrong.

> *And do not be conformed to this world, but be transformed by the renewing of your mind, so that you may prove what the will of God is, that which is good and acceptable and perfect.* (Romans 12:2 NASB)

I will later talk about other areas that God proves to be sin through His Word. It is important that you do not close your eyes but that you are open, so God can take you to a higher level in holiness and purity.

> *… And find out what pleases the Lord. Have nothing to do with the fruitless deeds of darkness, but rather expose them."* (Ephesians 5:10-11 NIV)

Throughout this whole book. I will try to create a boundary between accidentally doing something wrong—sin that has not yet been revealed as sin—and doing something that you know is wrong, thus, living in "conscious" or "willful" sin.

4

FEAR OF THE LORD

The word *eusebeia* is translated as "godliness." For example, in 1 Timothy 6:3 (NASB): "*If anyone advocates a different doctrine and does not agree with sound words, those of our Lord Jesus Christ, and with the doctrine conforming to godliness ...*" This word can also be translated as "piety," "holiness," or "respectful fear of God." In another place it says:

> *Since, then, we know what it is to fear the Lord, we try to persuade others ...*" (2 Corinthians 5:11 NIV)

Here, "to fear the Lord" comes from the word *phobos*. This word means "to get fear or terror." We can translate the verse this way: "Because of fear of the Lord, we try to persuade men."

What kind of fear of the Lord is it that I have experienced? It is not the kind of fear that is in the world. For example, I do not go around in fear that someone will come and kill me. Neither do I think that I am not good enough or that I cannot live up to this and that. It is more like enormous honor and respect and, at the same time, fear toward God because of who He is—a Holy God. He is also our good and loving Father. It is this kind of respect and fear that makes one look up to Him and wish to please Him. You love what God loves and hate what He hates (Proverbs 8:13). Therefore, you do not want, or dare, to do anything that God hates. Fear of the Lord makes you hate fornication, lies, immorality, and so on, and fear of the Lord makes you love what God loves—holiness, purity, helping people, and witnessing about Him (John 14:15; 2. Corinthians 5:11; 1 Timothy 6:14).

Through Him

How do you get this fear of the Lord? You begin by discovering who God really is. I began to experience some of it when I heard a series of tapes that, among other things, talked about the reality of hell and fear of the Lord. The speaker was a pastor from the USA. It was so radical in all ways.

The message was not made soft. He called sin by its right name and taught that it separates us from God. I began to see a side of God I had never known before. He started to work in me, and I began to read and study what the Bible really says about Him and how it all fits together. I realized that if we, as Christians, live in conscious sin, we are not any better positioned than people in the world who do not know Jesus. It created fear of the Lord and a whole new sharpness against sin in my life.

> *His divine power has given us everything we need for life and godliness through our knowledge of him who called us by his own glory and goodness.* (2 Peter 1:3 NIV)

As you see, it is through gaining knowledge of Him as He really is that we will fear the Lord. I will mention various things in this book that will let God's Word show you Who He really is.

You might believe that someone writing about sin in such a radical way could create a wrong kind of fear inside of a person. But as long as it is God's Word we hold onto, then it should not be softened, no matter how radical it is, because God's Word is truth. If there is a truth therein that we have not yet obtained, then isn't it about time to get hold of it before it's too late in some areas? Let me say this again: *As long as it is God's Word, it cannot be too radical!* Of course, it has to be said in a *right* way because, if it is not said out of love, it can create something wrong that God never intended.

My only wish is that people will be set free, as I have experienced. We should not hold back or soften the Word of God out of fear that people might misinterpret our words and get hurt or be turned back to the bondage of the Law. We have held back in the past, and it resulted in nothing good. The Word of God needs to be preached because it is the truth. Look at the life of Jesus. People mocked Him and were angry at Him because He spoke the truth to them. Almost all of His disciples left Him once, not because He had done something wrong, but because He spoke the Word of God radically, as it is. He spoke the truth to the people, and it hurt:

> *As the living Father sent Me, and I live because of the Father, so he who feeds on Me will live because of Me. This is the bread which came down from heaven—not as your fathers ate the manna, and are dead. He who eats this bread will live forever.*
>
> *These things He said in the synagogue as He taught in Capernaum. Therefore many of His disciples, when they heard this, said, "This is a hard saying; who can understand it?" When Jesus knew in Himself that His disciples complained about this, He said to them, "Does this offend you? What then if you should see the Son of Man ascend where He was before? It is the Spirit who gives life; the flesh profits nothing. The words that I speak to you are spirit, and they are life. But there are some of you who do not believe." For Jesus knew from the beginning who they were who did not believe, and who would betray Him. And He said, "Therefore I have said to you that no one can come to Me unless it has been granted to him by My Father."*
>
> *From that time many of His disciples went back and walked with Him no more. Then Jesus said to the twelve, "Do you also want to go away?" But Simon Peter answered Him, "Lord, to whom shall we go? You have the words of eternal life."* (John 6:57-68 NKJV)

Here, we see that even Jesus would not, and could not, satisfy all people. He spoke the truth even if there were some who did not like it and went their way. Although He knew that they grumbled about the things He said, He continued speaking. Finally, almost everyone left. Isn't it about time we stopped trying to satisfy people by only telling them what they want to hear? It is only the truth that sets people free.

We can also see that in the story of the rich young ruler:

> *"When the young man heard this, he went away sad, because he had great wealth."* (Matthew 19:22 NIV)

Here, Jesus did not give the young man the answer that he wanted to hear. Jesus did not hold Himself back from speaking truth, so why should we hold back for fear of offending or hurting people? Of course, some will get hurt, but if we speak the truth of the Word, many more will be set free.

As we continue teaching the fear of the Lord, we must let God reveal Himself to us through His Word. We must be open and willing to let His Word change us to be more like Him, even if it defies some of the things we are used to hearing or seems too radical and too intrusive for us. Our desire as Christians should be to be more like Him and to live the life that God has for us.

5

GRACE

Grace is a very important part of our Christian life. Without grace, there would be no hope for us. We would walk around in constant fear and wait for our deserved punishment. I will not use a lot of space to say what it means to be saved by grace because I am certain that we have often heard about it. However, I will try to show another thing that grace does for us.

> *But now a righteousness from God, apart from law, has been made known, to which the Law and the Prophets testify. This righteousness from God comes through faith in Jesus Christ to all who believe. There is no difference, for all have sinned and fall short of the glory of God, and are justified freely by his grace through the redemption that came by Christ Jesus. (Romans 3:21-24 NIV)*

The words used here, "justified freely," probably give the best description of grace. We are saved by grace, not because we are so good, not because we have done all kinds of things. It is not by living up to the Law that we get saved, but by His grace we have freely gained access to God through our faith in Jesus.

> *Now when a man works, his wages are not credited to him as a gift, but as an obligation. However, to the man who does not work but trusts God who justifies the wicked, his faith is credited as righteousness. (Romans 4:4-5 NIV)*

These verses are saying that, if you work, you get paid for your work. However, we have received salvation through our faith in Jesus, not as payment for something that we have done. This is the great difference between Law and grace.

For the law was given through Moses; grace and truth came through Jesus Christ. (John 1:17 NIV)

The Law came with rules and commandments that one should keep, but, as we know, no person has been justified by the Law (Romans 3:20; 11:6). That is why God had to create a "better" way, so that we did not have to do a lot of things to get saved. That better way is the way of faith (Romans 4:13).

Someone may ask, "Why are you now saying that it is by faith and not by deeds? That is exactly the opposite of what you have written before." No, what I want to show you is that there is a difference between coming to God and living with Him. As I have been saying all the time, we can only come to God if we see ourself as a sinner, come to repentance, and believe on Jesus. Then we can receive forgiveness and eternal life. We are saved by grace. I do not wish to go back to the Law where we have to do all the right things to get saved. God has once and for all paved a much better way through Jesus, and that is what we should hold on to. Without Jesus, there is no salvation. We cannot possibly live righteously enough to earn our salvation. However, after we are saved, things are a bit different.

People should also be cleansed

Let me give you a little example. God says that we should be fishers of men (Matthew 4:19), which means that we should "catch" people into the Kingdom of God. Just like with fish, you cannot cleanse people of the scales and bad "guts" before you have "caught" them. As sinners, we are undeservedly saved by grace through Jesus Christ and not by keeping the Law. When we were "caught," we were still dirty and sinful. The Word says that God is holy, and that is why we should also be holy (1 Peter 1:16). When we give our life to God through Jesus Christ and are brought "ashore," He will begin to cleanse us because He cannot have fellowship with sin. As long as we are willing to let God come with "the knife" and "rip us up," He can come all the way inside with His

Spirit and remove all the filth, and then we are living in grace. So, when God points to some dirt in our lives, we must open ourselves and let Him cleanse it. It is so important that we do not abuse God's grace because if one is not willing to let God come through, it will go wrong.

Beloved, while I was very diligent to write to you concerning our common salvation, I found it necessary to write to you exhorting you to contend earnestly for the faith which was once for all delivered to the saints. For certain men have crept in unnoticed, who long ago were marked out for this condemnation, ungodly men, who turn the grace of our God into lewdness and deny the only Lord God and our Lord Jesus Christ. (Jude 1:3-4 NKJV)

Here, he speaks about some who turn the grace of God into lewdness. He also talks about some who deny Jesus Christ, but we do not do that. As you see, it is possible to abuse God's grace. We can perceive that around us. I had done the same in some areas before I experienced the fear of the Lord that I am writing about. I did things that I knew were wrong, but I thought that God is gracious. I was like that in some areas, and there are, unfortunately, many today who are also like that.

"God *is* a gracious God." Yes, He is, but be careful not to abuse His grace. God forgives sin in our lives when we come to Him, but we should not play with sin by thinking, for example, "God is gracious, so I can always go to Him later and receive forgiveness. There is no reason for me to throw out my TV, even though I see some wrong things over and over again. I will just ask for forgiveness later." It is wrong to have this attitude. If you are like that, then watch out because, one day, it will go wrong. Let us not insult the Spirit of grace (Hebrews 10:29).

Shall we remain in the flesh?

What shall we say, then? Shall we go on sinning so that grace may increase? By no means! We are those who have died to sin; how can we live in it any longer? (Romans 6:1-2 NIV)

As you see here, Paul asks one of the frequently asked questions that comes directly from the flesh trying to find any little door that is just a little bit open so that sin can creep in and find its fulfillment. Paul answers, *"By no means!"* You can almost hear him saying, "What are you thinking about?" He continues, *"We died to sin; how can we live in it any longer?"* The answer he gives is understandable, is it not? He says clearly that we should not have anything in common with the flesh, not even if we are under grace. Why?

Therefore there is now no condemnation for those who are in Christ Jesus. For the law of the Spirit of life in Christ Jesus has set you free from the law of sin and of death. For what the Law could not do, weak as it was through the flesh, God did: sending His own Son in the likeness of sinful flesh and as an offering for sin, He condemned sin in the flesh, so that the requirement of the Law might be fulfilled in us, who do not walk according to the flesh but according to the Spirit. For those who are according to the flesh set their minds on the things of the flesh, but those who are according to the Spirit, the things of the Spirit. For the mind set on the flesh is death, but the mind set on the Spirit is life and peace, because the mind set on the flesh is hostile toward God; for it does not subject itself to the law of God, for it is not even able to do so, and those who are in the flesh cannot please God.

So then, brethren, we are under obligation, not to the flesh, to live according to the flesh—for if you are living according to the flesh, you must die; but if by the Spirit you are putting to death the deeds of the body, you will live. (Romans 8:1-8, 12-13 NASB)

Paul says clearly that the mind set on the flesh is hostile toward God, and if we, as brothers of Jesus, Christians, who live by grace, live in obedience to the flesh, then we shall die. But, hallelujah, he also says that with the Spirit's help, we can put to death the deeds of the flesh and live. Let us see what those deeds are:

Now the deeds of the flesh are evident, which are: immorality, impurity, sensuality, idolatry, sorcery, enmities, strife, jealousy, outbursts of anger, disputes, dissensions, factions, envying, drunkenness, carousing, and things like these, of which I forewarn you, just as I have forewarned you, that those who practice such things will not inherit the Kingdom of God. (Galatians 5:19-21 NASB)

Here, we see what the deeds of the flesh are. Notice the ending of verse 21, *"I forewarn you, just as I have forewarned you, that those who practice such things will not inherit the Kingdom of God."* If there is anything that is radical, then this is it. Paul mentions that if we, as

Christian brothers and sisters who live by grace, live according to the flesh, we shall die. Yes, he even says that he has mentioned it before, so it is not just another quick remark.

Grace teaches us

Let us go back to grace for a second, and later we will go deeper into what the deeds of the flesh are. Romans 8:12 says that with the Spirit's help, we should put the flesh to death. Another Scripture that explains this quite well is:

> For the grace of God that brings salvation has appeared to all men. It teaches us to say "No" to ungodliness and worldly passions, and to live self-controlled, upright and godly lives in this present age. (Titus 2:11-12 NIV)

Here, it is written that grace teaches as well. It teaches us to say no to ungodliness and worldly passions and to live a self-controlled and upright life. It was sin that separated us from God before we received Jesus, and it is the same sin that will separate us from God today, after we have received grace and salvation in Jesus. However, the big difference is that we have the grace that helps us live upright lives so that we do not have to fall into sin again and again. This is the big difference between we who are saved and those who do not know God. Through baptism, we are delivered from sin. The power of sin is broken in our life. Apart from that, we have the grace that teaches us to say no to sin and the world. It helps us live a self-controlled, upright, and godly life in this world. Just think about it: by the help of grace and God's Spirit, it is possible to live in purity, free from sin. Hallelujah! When I realized this, something was set free inside of me, and I felt that I had already overcome sin. I saw that by the grace of God, it was possible for me to be free from any bondage to sin that I had before. Now, with the help of God's grace, we can live up to the Ten Commandments and all of the other things that people had been powerless over before the time of Jesus.

In the next chapter, you will be able to read more about what it means to overcome sin. Through Christ, we are bought into a life of victory over sin. Some people may argue, "No, you must be mistaken. We cannot live in victory over sin. Like it says in Romans 7, sin has power over us."

Let's take a closer look at it, and see what God's Word says about that.

6

ARE WE BOUND BY SIN?

My dear children, I write this to you so that you will not sin. But if anybody does sin, we have one who speaks to the Father in our defense—Jesus Christ, the Righteous One. (1 John 2:1 NIV)

It is so important for us to understand that our goal is not to fall and receive forgiveness afterward. The goal is that we not fall at all. However, if we do fall, there is forgiveness for us. Therefore:

I do not understand what I do. For what I want to do I do not do, but what I hate I do. And if I do what I do not want to do, I agree that the law is good. As it is, it is no longer I myself who do it, but it is sin living in me. I know that nothing good lives in me, that is, in my sinful nature. For I have the desire to do what is good, but I cannot carry it out. For what I do is not the good I want to do; no, the evil I do not want to do—this I keep on doing. Now if I do what I do not want to do, it is no longer I who do it, but it is sin living in me that does it. (Romans 7:15-20 NIV)

This is a well-known part of the Bible. These verses are often used as an excuse for one's sinful acts. We should never take a few verses out of context and build a teaching on them. Unfortunately, that has been done many times with these verses.

Remember that God's Word says, *"Every matter must be established by the testimony of two or three witnesses"* (2 Corinthians 13:1 NIV),

43

and, *"The sum of Your word is truth"* (Psalm 119:160 NASB). If we look at what we have just read and say that it is normal to sin because we are under sin, and we cannot help it anyway, then we are wrong. It does not match with the sum of God's Word. God's Word clearly says that the power of sin is broken over us who live with Jesus. If we are in Him, we have power over sin. You may argue, "But these verses clearly tell us that it is sin that acts in him, and he cannot help it." Yes, it is true, but these verses explain Paul's situation before he received Jesus. Without Jesus, sin has power, and that was exactly why Jesus came— to break the power of sin.

> *He who sins is of the devil, for the devil has sinned from the beginning. For this purpose the Son of God was manifested, that He might destroy the works of the devil.* (1 John 3:8 NKJV)

You could say that the headline for the verses that we read before in Romans 7:15-20, where Paul says that sin has power over us, can be found here:

> *For when we were in the flesh, the sinful passions which were aroused by the law were at work in our members to bear fruit to death.* (Romans 7:5 NKJV)

He speaks about the time when he was in the flesh, before he got to know Jesus, and when he was still a sinner. We see, therefore, that we are no longer sold to be subject to sin, as we were before.

> *For we know that the Law is spiritual, but I am of flesh, sold into bondage to sin.* (Romans 7:14 NASB)

Now, since we live with Jesus, we are free from sin, as it says in the previous chapter:

> *But God be thanked that though you were slaves of sin, yet you obeyed from the heart that form of doctrine to which you were delivered. And having been set free from sin, you became slaves of righteousness.* (Romans 6:17-18 NKJV)

> *But now having been set free from sin, and having become slaves of God, you have your fruit to holiness, and the end, everlasting life.* (Romans 6:22 NKJV)

Sin has only that power over you that you allow it to have. Because of Jesus we are free from sin and its power.

Romans

Some time ago I began a study of the Book of Romans, particularly chapters six through eight. In Romans 7:7, Paul speaks of the Law and its affect on his old, unregenerate man—before he was born again in Jesus. He says the Law is good because it revealed his sin nature. After speaking of the conflict that the two natures cause, he says:

O wretched man that I am! Who will deliver me from this body of death? I thank God—through Jesus Christ our Lord! So then, with the mind I myself serve the law of God, but with the flesh the law of sin. (Romans 7:24-25 NKJV)

Paul asks who could rescue him from this body of sin that is destined for death. Then we come to chapter eight and read that Jesus can set us free.

Therefore there is now no condemnation for those who are in Christ Jesus. For the law of the Spirit of life in Christ Jesus has set you free from the law of sin and of death. (Romans 8:2 NASB)

In Jesus, we are set free from sin, and there is no condemnation in Him. Everything is now total victory! Jesus does not just give us victory. He *IS* our Victory!

During the time of my study of Romans, we were going to visit some of my family who were living on the opposite side of Denmark. On the way there, I felt led to especially study Romans 6 through 8. It was not long before I realized that Romans 8, verses 1 and 4 go together, so it actually says:

Therefore there is now no condemnation for those who are in Christ Jesus ... those who do not walk according to the flesh but according to the Spirit." (Romans 8:1, 4 NASB)

This Scripture struck me because there are many people today who immediately start quoting Romans 8:1 if they experience anything that feels like condemnation. Instead of listening to God and examining themselves to see if they may be "in the flesh," they use Romans 8:1 as a form of denial of the sin in their lives. God often speaks conviction to our hearts. If we have been born again and continue to walk according to the flesh, or continue to live in sin, then we will experience condemnation in our hearts. That condemnation should make us repent for the sin and receive forgiveness. Then we will be set free from the condemnation and guilt because we do not walk according to the flesh anymore. The Scripture that says there is no condemnation should not make us close our ears but, instead, listen to what God might say to us in our cleansed conscience.

When we arrived at my family's home, I saw a Christian magazine on the table. I picked it up to see if there was anything exciting in it. On one of the first pages, an article caught my eye. A young man wrote that, as a Christian, one lives a double life because of all the wrong things that are done. He quoted the Scripture from Romans 7 that we just read and continued saying: "All week long, you do a lot of sinful things, but on Sundays you can stand in the church as God's child." I thought: "What is going on? This cannot be true." I continued reading, and he said that he, as a Christian, experienced condemnation almost all the time, and it was difficult for him to feel righteous. That is why he quoted the Scripture from Romans 8:1, which says that there is no condemnation in Jesus. As I read that article, it did not sound as if the writer knew Jesus or lived with Him as His child. Of course, you will experience condemnation if you live in sin. I prayed quietly: "Oh, God, You have to do something. There are so many people in the churches today who are being deceived, and if something does not happen soon, they will be lost."

It is finished

What Jesus did on the cross is finished. He won a victory over sin and death once and for all (1 Corinthians 15:54-55; 1 John 5:4). He paid the price so that sin would not have power over us, but that we would have power over sin because of what He did.

God's Word reveals the freedom that Christ has given us. Let's look at what Jesus says about the Law in His Sermon on the Mount in Matthew 5.

Jesus states (v. 17) that He did not come to abolish the Law but to fulfill it. Then He repeats five times in this chapter, "You have heard that it was said …" He is telling the people that they have heard that the Law of Moses says this and that. He mentions five different requirements for living under the Law: You shall not kill, you shall not commit adultery, you shall not give false testimony, an eye for an eye and a tooth for a tooth, and you shall love your neighbor and hate your enemy. Then Jesus speaks of some of the Laws and Commandments in the Old Covenant that He came to fulfill. If we read what He says about the different Laws, we can see that He makes them stricter instead of breaking them. He wants a higher standard, elevated from flesh to spirit.

It says in the Law that Moses brought down from the mountain that you shall not murder, but now Jesus says that if you are angry with your brother—some original texts include "for no reason" or "without a cause"—you will be in danger of the judgment. If you say "you fool," you will be in danger of hell fire.

Therefore, the Bible says that if you say "you fool" to a brother or if you are angry with your brother for no reason, then you shall be found guilty. This shows that sin is not something we should treat lightly. That is why it is so important that we test ourselves all the time. If there is someone you are angry with or someone you have not forgiven, then hurry up and repent. Do not go to hell just because you are too proud to forgive or because you think it is not you who should ask for forgiveness. It is very serious and not something we should play with.

Jesus says in Matthew 5:27 that you have heard it was said to those of old, "You shall not commit adultery." Committing adultery in the Old Covenant meant you had sex with someone to whom you were not married, but look how it is written in the New Covenant:

"But I tell you that anyone who looks at a woman lustfully has already committed adultery with her in his heart." (Matthew 5:28 NIV)

We see that, now, just looking at a woman lustfully is committing adultery in the heart. This also applies if a single person looks lustfully at their boyfriend or girlfriend. It is sin to lust after them outside of marriage. "Dating" someone does not mean the two of you are already one. Becoming one is done through covenant with God. Your boyfriend or girlfriend does not belong to you before you are married. So hurry up and repent, if this is what you do.

You might argue, "But it is not easy. When we kiss, we get a desire for each other." Yes, but neither does the Bible say that you should kiss each other when you are dating. Kissing arouses passions. It awakens a desire and a lust that is sin as long as you are not married. This is something about which we have a totally wrong picture in our churches. We play with sin! If we do not stop and repent, it will go wrong because sin separates us from God. If you desire someone who is not your wife, you live in fornication, and fornicators have no inheritance in the Kingdom of God (Ephesians 5:5). So if you are living with a desire or lust like that, you need to repent.

> "If your right eye causes you to sin, pluck it out and cast it from you; for it is more profitable for you that one of your members perish, than for your whole body to be cast into hell. And if your right hand causes you to sin, cut it off and cast it from you; for it is more profitable for you that one of your members perish, than for your whole body to be cast into hell." (Matthew 5:29-30 NKJV)

We must really start to see how radical God's Word is. Something like this creates godliness. Jesus says also in verse 20 that "unless your righteousness exceeds the righteousness of the scribes and Pharisees, you will by no means enter the kingdom of heaven" (Matthew 5:20). We should not play with sin but pursue to live rightly.

Be perfect

As I mentioned before, there is hope. Before God opened my eyes and this true fear of the Lord entered into my life, I fell again and again by looking at something I should not look at. But now there is victory. For example, I do not need to stay home to avoid looking at a girl and falling. The temptation and desire that had the chance to come through in the past does not get the opportunity to do so now.

You may say that "God surely cannot mean that we have to keep everything that is written in this Scripture, that we should not look lustfully at someone, that we must not be angry with a brother, and that we have to love our enemies, and so on." I can tell you that it is really not as difficult as you may think. When we are walking in the Spirit and living close to Him with true fear of the Lord in our lives, then He helps us. It is explained in 2 Peter 2 that if He saved Noah, a preacher of righteousness, from the flood and righteous Lot from the destruction of Sodom and Gomorrah ...

> ... then the Lord knows how to deliver the godly out of temptations and to reserve the unjust under punishment for the day of judgment ... (2 Peter 2:9 NKJV)

Hallelujah, God can deliver us from the temptations so that we will not fall but live as Jesus commands us at the end of Matthew 5:

> "Be perfect, therefore, as your heavenly Father is perfect." (Matthew 5:48 NIV)

It also says:

> He who says, "I know Him," and does not keep His commandments, is a liar, and the truth is not in him. (1 John 2:4 NKJV)

Are we sinners?

In the Bible, it looks like it is actually possible to live without sin. "That is not true," you might say. "All of us are sinners. Read yourself what it says in John 8:7, where there are some who want to stone a woman taken in the act of adultery. Jesus says that the one without sin should throw the first stone. And we see that no one throws because they are all in sin." Yes, it is true that they were all in sin, but that took place before Jesus died and showed His great mercy for us by winning an eternal victory over sin. This victory applies to you and me, so we can be free from sin.

Another question might be: "What about 1 John 1:8?" John says, "If we claim to be without sin, we deceive ourselves and the truth is not in us" (1 John 1:8 NIV).

Remember that "the sum of God's Word is truth." In the previous verse John says:

> But if we walk in the light, as he is in the light, we have fellowship with one another, and the blood of Jesus, his Son, purifies us from all sin. (1 John 1:7 NIV)

Jesus purifies us from all sin if we walk in the light. If He purifies us from all sin, then we have no sin.

"But even Paul says that he is a sinner."

It is a trustworthy statement, deserving full acceptance, that Christ Jesus came into the world to save sinners, among whom I am foremost of all. (1 Timothy 1:15 NASB)

Yes, Paul was a sinner, even the foremost of all sinners, as he said, because he had persecuted the church of God (1 Corinthians 15:9). However, he states in the very same verse that Jesus came into the world to save sinners. What he says is in the past tense. The word translated as "am" in the original text can also be translated as "was" or "have been." In this context, "was" is the best word that can be used for this translation because Jesus has already saved him. Why should Jesus come into the world to save sinners if we are still sinners after receiving Him? Therefore, the life that God has for us is a life of victory. Yes, we were sinners, but not anymore, if we do not walk in sin anymore. If we do that, then we are still sinners.

John also states:

We know that no one who is born of God sins; but He who was born of God keeps him, and the evil one does not touch him. (1 John 5:18 NASB)

We read here that Jesus can and will keep us so that we will not sin. In 1 Corinthians 10:13, Paul says that God will not allow us to be tempted beyond our ability. What he means here is that, because of Jesus' victory, we as Christians can always resist any temptation. We will never be confronted with a temptation that is so big we cannot resist it in Jesus. Therefore, it seems possible not to fall into sin.

No temptation has overtaken you except such as is common to man; but God is faithful, who will not allow you to be tempted beyond what you are able, but with the temptation will also make the way of escape, that you may be able to bear it (1 Corinthians 10:13 NKJV).

A few words of wisdom

Come to your senses and stop sinning ... (1 Cor. 15:34a NLT)

As obedient children, do not conform to the evil desires you had when you lived in ignorance. But just as he who called you is holy, so be holy in all you do; for it is written: "Be holy, because I am holy." (1 Peter 1:14-16 NIV)

Therefore do not let sin reign in your mortal body so that you obey its lusts. (Romans 6:12 NASB)

You might think: "It is easier said than done. 'Let not sin reign.' It cannot be done." Yes, it can. In the next chapters, I will show you how and what it takes.

7

DO NOT LET SIN RULE

If you do not want sin to rule, it is important to have the right attitude toward it. You must hate sin because if you love it, you will never become free from it. "Love sin? Who loves sin?" Let me tell you about a testimony that I once heard.

There was a man who had progressively attended church for some years. He smoked and had tried almost everything to become free. Many different preachers prayed for him, but it did not help. He was not set free. One day, his friend became a Christian. The strange thing was that his friend was set free from cigarettes the same day he became a Christian. The man who still smoked said to God, "What is happening? I have been attending church for so many years. I have been prayed for by many different people, and still I have not been set free. Then comes my friend, who has just been saved, and he becomes free right away." He was about to light a cigarette when God spoke to him: "The reason you have not been set free is that you love your sin." He stopped, looked at his cigarette, and thought, "Yes, it is true. I have loved sin." After that, he got angry with his sin and threw his cigarette away. Then he became free, and from that day, he smoked no more.

This testimony really pushes the right buttons. There are so many people in churches today who walk in sin and do not feel they can be set free, but the problem is that they love sin. God does not come and make you suddenly hate sin and become free. It begins with you. You must come to the point where you hate sin so much that you think it is disgusting and sickening.

"Hate what is evil; cling to what is good" (Romans 12:9 NIV). Paul is speaking to Christians. If you live like some of those he mentions here, it doesn't matter whether you speak in tongues, pray, read the Bible, are a pastor, or experience signs and wonders. You are not going to inherit the Kingdom of God. Yes, this creates the fear of the Lord, but that is what is needed.

Before we move on, it is important to understand that the standard by which we are supposed to live is God's and not those of humans. We are too busy looking up to other people and comparing ourselves to them. In some areas, it is all right, but do not take it for granted that people are living a holy and pure life because they are being used by God. God does not withdraw His anointing and calling (Romans 11:29). Thus, even the most anointed person in the country can be living in conscious sin and be on the road to hell while producing signs and wonders in ministry.

If there is someone you look up to because he is anointed, and you see him do wrong things, do not think that if he can do this and that, it must be all right for you to do it, too. No, let us not look upon other people as the standards for our lives. Look to God and His Word to see how we should live. Imagine that you start doing the same sinful things you see other people doing. It does not help you in the Judgment that the person who does that is a pastor or someone who experiences power and miracles.

If you are living in conscious and willful sin and do not care what God is telling you about it, you will perish even if you experience signs and wonders. You can read in John 12:6 that Judas Iscariot, a disciple of Jesus, was a thief because he stole from the money box. Thieves will not inherit the Kingdom of God, but we still see in Matthew 10:1 that Jesus gave him authority over unclean spirits and power to heal in the same manner as the other disciples. We can also look at Samson. He lived in fornication with a prostitute, but the power of God was still upon him (Judges 16). Just because people are walking in the power of God, it does not necessarily mean that we must live like they do. We should live only as God says.

The Bible is extremely radical

*Now the works of the flesh are evident, which are: adultery, forni-
cation, uncleanness, lewdness, idolatry, sorcery, hatred, contentions,
jealousies, outbursts of wrath, selfish ambitions, dissensions, heresies,
envy, murders, drunkenness, revelries, and the like; of which I tell you
beforehand, just as I also told you in time past, that those who
practice such things will not inherit the Kingdom of God. (Galatians
5:19-21 NKJV)*

It is very important that we live in righteousness. This strong
Scripture is written for Christians, so it is about those of us who attend
church and know Jesus. Let us be changed and not practice such things,
so we will not miss salvation. Although 1 Timothy 1:10 says almost the
same, liars are also included there. It is not something to play with.

I will tell you a little testimony before we move on. One day, I was
picking up my wife at the office where she was working. When she
stepped into the car and we began the drive home, she suddenly said:
"I wonder if I'm going to get fired."

I exclaimed: "What? Are you going to get fired? Why?"

She then told me that there had suddenly come a man to whom
they owed money. Her boss had hurried to say to her that if the man
asked if she had transferred some money to him, she should just say:
"Yes, I have done that." This was not true, so she refused as the man
came in. She did not want to lie.

Later on, the man asked my wife if she had transferred the money
to him, and she told him the truth: "No, I have not, and I have not been
told to do so, either." She got pretty nervous about what her boss would
say when he heard this. When we got home, she called her boss because
she had not spoken to him since. She told him that it was, of course,
up to him what he was going to do, but he could not make her lie. Her
boss said it was all right.

I thought she handled the situation very well. My wife is so cool.
She did the only right thing. We must not lie! If you are living in a lie
today, then hurry up and come out with the truth. Remember who the
Bible says is the father of lies. It is the devil, and if we as Christians lie,
then we are his children (John 8:44).

As obedient children, do not conform to the evil desires you had when you lived in ignorance. But just as he who called you is holy, so be holy in all you do; for it is written: "Be holy, because I am holy." Since you call on a Father who judges each man's work impartially, live your lives as strangers here in reverent fear. (1 Peter 1:14-17 NIV)

We are not going to begin living in the fear of the Lord before we start to see sin as something that separates us from God. We need to see that if we allow sin, then we cannot have fellowship with God and receive our reward. Instead, we will be judged. Remember, however, what I have written earlier: There is hope, for grace helps us and teaches us. As long as we are willing to let God come through to us, there is grace over our lives.

Do not play with sin

Here is a section that can give you something to think about. I have never heard this preached in any church, but it is a part of God's Word.

For I do not want you to be ignorant of the fact, brothers, that our forefathers were all under the cloud and that they all passed through the sea. They were all baptized into Moses in the cloud and in the sea. They all ate the same spiritual food and drank the same spiritual drink; for they drank from the spiritual rock that accompanied them, and that rock was Christ. Nevertheless, God was not pleased with most of them; their bodies were scattered over the desert. Now these things occurred as examples to keep us from setting our hearts on evil things as they did. Do not be idolaters, as some of them were; as it is written: "The people sat down to eat and drink and got up to indulge in pagan revelry." We should not commit sexual immorality, as some of them did—and in one day twenty-three thousand of them died. We should not test the Lord, as some of them did—and were killed by snakes. And do not grumble, as some of them did—and were killed by the destroying angel. These things happened to them as examples and were written down as warnings for us, on whom the fulfillment of the ages has come. So, if you think you are standing firm, be careful that you don't fall! No temptation has seized you except what is common to man. And God is faithful; he will not let you be tempted beyond what you can bear. But when you are tempted, he will also provide a way out so that you can stand up under it. (1 Corinthians 10:1-13 NIV)

We have heard the last two verses about temptations many times, but I do not think that we have often heard the whole context in our churches today. Why? Because Christians have slackened their resolve to be holy as He is holy. We allow sin. We do not dare to tell the truth because we might hurt somebody. That must come to an end! Let the truth come out so that people can be set free. Let God's Word work inside of us. Let this which we have just read be a warning to us so that we do not set our hearts to do evil.

> *For if we sin willfully after we have received the knowledge of the truth, there no longer remains a sacrifice for sins, but a certain fearful expectation of judgment, and fiery indignation which will devour the adversaries. Anyone who has rejected Moses' law dies without mercy on the testimony of two or three witnesses. Of how much worse punishment, do you suppose, will he be thought worthy who has trampled the Son of God underfoot, counted the blood of the covenant by which he was sanctified a common thing, and insulted the Spirit of grace? For we know Him who said, "Vengeance is Mine, I will repay," says the Lord. And again, "The LORD will judge His people." It is a fearful thing to fall into the hands of the living God.* (Hebrews 10:26-31 NKJV)

This is strong! If we sin willfully after we have received knowledge of the truth, there no longer remains a sacrifice for sins. Such a Scripture pricks the heart. If you are thinking: "It is me. I have sinned wilfully," then I just want to say that I have also done that, but after I received the knowledge that I am presenting in this book, I have not been living in conscious sin like before. Personally, I have come to the point where this Scripture applies to me. I believe that if I keep on living in willful sin, I can lose my salvation, and then it will be too late. You might try throwing a lot of Scriptures at me, but remember that the sum of God's Word is the truth. While I have been trying to prepare you for this throughout this whole book, I, at the same time, have shown what this recognition has done in me: I have become free from sin.

Throughout this whole book, I have been trying to draw a clear line between sinning on purpose and doing something that is sin. I still might do something that is sin because I am not perfect, but I am working on it. God is still working in me. He is showing me things all the time that I should work on. Sanctification does not happen in a moment. It is a process that takes time. That is why it is important to let God work in us all the time so that we can distinguish between good and evil.

> *But solid food is for the mature, who by constant use have trained themselves to distinguish good from evil. (Hebrews 5:14 NIV)*

I know today where I fell before, and I know what can make it happen again. However, it will not happen because I will not allow the flesh to take over. I know, for example, that impure sexual thoughts used to be a problem, and that is why, today, I do not look at underwear commercials or other things that can awaken the flesh inside of me. Sin is not something we should play with. Remember, we are going to live forever, either in heaven or in hell.

Cut it off and throw it away

> *And if your right hand* [friends, TV, Internet, alcohol, etc.] *causes you to sin, cut it off and throw it away. It is better for you to lose one part of your body* [friends, TV, Internet, alcohol, etc.] *than for your whole body to go into hell. (Matthew 5:30 NIV)* [Bracketed words are mine]

It is incredibly important that you not have an open back door for sin. For example, why do you have satellite TV with a lot of programs if the only thing they show is junk? "But I am not watching it." Then why do you have it? Let me try to explain what I mean.

If you, for example, have a good day and feel that God is near, then you do not think of doing anything sinful. You are very sharp against sin. If you are going to watch a movie, and there comes a scene that is not the best, then you hurry up and fast-forward, while you are looking away. You absolutely do not want to look at something wrong because you do not want to have anything to do with sin. After you have seen the movie you just bought, you put it back on the shelf and think: "Good movie. There was just one scene that was not so good, but I am strong, so I did not see it because there is victory." However, after five or six days you come home from work in a really bad mood. Perhaps the boss has been criticizing you the whole day, and then you come home and everything irritates you. You walk around, mad at this and that, and you put aside all these things with God. In the meantime, while you are feeling sorry for yourself, you see the movie on the shelf where you placed it. Suddenly, you are not as strong as you were a couple of days before. You turn on the movie, and instead of fast-forwarding past the naughty scene, you are now fast forwarding toward it.

I know this is something many people know. Maybe not the TV part, but what about the Internet, magazines, music, friends, alcohol, chocolate cake, or other things? Are you aware that your home is your church? What would you do if Jesus came and said that He would like to be a guest in your house today? Do you have some things that are wrong? For your own sake, throw them away. I think that we as Christians could benefit from taking a big black trash bag and cleaning out our homes, so we can get the back door closed to Satan.

I can say that our home is clean. I do not have anything that can make me stumble. However, I do have access to the Internet since I have a website about Jesus. I know there are many who have fallen into sin because of the Internet. There is so much junk there, and it is so unbelievably easy to get hold of it at any time. That is why I have decided that if I just once surf on one of the wrong pages, I cannot keep my access to the Internet anymore, which also means that I will lose my Christian website. Sin must have a consequence! "Yeah, yeah, I have heard that one before. I have also said it once, and it did not hold." Make a deal with a friend, so that he gets into your computer from time to time and checks what pages you have been visiting. Then you cannot just visit some pages without your friend knowing it. It is important to remember that God sees everything, including our sins. If it is you I am talking about here, then repent and confess it to someone else before the flames of hell start to devour you. This can sound really extreme, but now is the time of grace. Tomorrow, it can be too late.

If you have true fear of the Lord in your life, it is not important to make such deals, but until you get it, it can be necessary. Having a good friend is worth gold. We all need a friend that we can trust and speak to if we experience a battle with sin, a friend who will not laugh at us but help us and stand together with us. In general, it is important to have friends. Choose the right ones that you will spend your time with.

If there are some who influence you in the wrong direction, then drop them, no matter how nice you think they are. God is big enough to find other friends for you. Do not have "bad" friends. They are not worth it. Do not lose your salvation because of bad influence from so-called friends, even if they call themselves Christians and attend church. I will address this later, but now let's go back to having the right attitude toward sin.

> *Pursue peace with all people, and holiness, without which no one will see the Lord: looking carefully lest anyone fall short of the grace of God; lest any root of bitterness springing up cause trouble, and by this many become defiled; lest there be any fornicator or profane person like Esau, who for one morsel of food sold his birthright. For you know that afterward, when he wanted to inherit the blessing, he was rejected, for he found no place for repentance, though he sought it diligently with tears.* (Hebrews 12:14-17 NKJV)

8

HATE SIN

... Hate what is evil; cling to what is good. (Romans 12:9 NIV)

*Do not conform any longer to the pattern of this world,
but be transformed..."* (Romans 12:2 NIV)

... make no provision for the flesh in regard to its lusts.
(Romans 13:14 NASB)

*Flee the evil desires of youth, and pursue righteousness,
faith, love and peace ...* (2 Timothy 2:22 NIV)

Here, we see what our attitude toward sin should be. As I said before, it is so important to have the right attitude. Sin is not something we should treat lightly. We should look at it as something destructive. We should not touch it or come near it. We must hate it together with what it brings, both in our own life and in our countries. Our attitude toward sin decides what kind of victory we will have over it. If we treat sin lightly, then we will not achieve victory over it. If we want to conquer sin, we have to come to hate it. Let us look at a section in the Bible that I think is really cool.

Now we exhort you, brethren, warn those who are unruly, comfort the fainthearted, uphold the weak, be patient with all. See that no one renders evil for evil to anyone, but always pursue what is good both for yourselves and for all. Rejoice always, pray without ceasing, in everything give thanks; for this is the will of God in Christ Jesus for you. Do not quench the Spirit. Do not despise prophecies. Test all things; hold fast what is good. Abstain from every form of evil. Now may the God of peace Himself sanctify you completely; and may your whole spirit, soul, and body be preserved blameless at the coming of our Lord Jesus Christ. (1 Thessalonians 5:14-23 NKJV)

There are many words of wisdom to grasp here, but let us look at the ending where it says: "Abstain from every form of evil." This is the attitude we are supposed to have because, like I said before, our attitude toward sin decides the victory we will have over it. And if we abstain from every form of evil, then: "The God of peace Himself will sanctify you completely; and your whole spirit, soul, and body will be preserved blameless at the coming of our Lord Jesus Christ." This is strong. It means that if we abstain from every form of evil, then God will preserve us blameless. It even says that our whole spirit, soul, and body will be preserved blameless! In other words, it is possible to be without sin because He preserves us, spirit, soul and body! The original text has a little "and" between the last two verses, so it should actually be: "Abstain from every form of evil, and now may the God of peace Himself sanctify you completely; and may your whole spirit, soul, and body be preserved blameless at the coming of our Lord Jesus Christ."

Make a choice

When we talk about abstaining from evil, we have to make some choices and get rid of things in our lives that have a bad influence on us. It can be friends, Internet, TV, etc. I find TV to be one of the huge problems among the people of God today. Not only does it steal a lot of time, but it also entices many to fall into sin and ruins families and homes. We have chosen not to have TV in our home, not because it is sin in itself, but because most of what comes out of it is sin. Its content is mostly nothing but fornication, murder, shameless talk, and much more, which God clearly states in His Word we should flee from. TV brings a lot of dullness and lukewarm attitudes into Christian homes. It has made people too dull to distinguish between good and evil.

TV is also one of the things that makes people fall into sin again and again. You see something wrong and repent, but soon you end up in the same sin again. I know it. Since I became a Christian, I have watched TV many times. One of the reasons I say many times is that I gave it up after a great meeting with God, and after a while, when the circumstances were a little tough, I plugged it in again. I did that many times, but now it is different because I have the fear of the Lord in my life, and because, today, I know that I should not play with sin.

Today, we have so much more time in my family for being together with people, more time for God, prayer, and reading His Word. Instead of spending an evening in front of the TV, I sit and read or do something else, and that is worth a fortune.

"Well, you could just turn off the TV." Yes, but I have to confess that I have not always been strong enough to do so. When we had a TV set, I felt that it was hard to spend time with God because, first, I had to see what was on TV. It is easy entertainment and pastime. Time is something we have all received equally. We all have 24 hours a day, and God wants us to manage that time properly.

"But it is not a sin to watch TV, is it? It is something everyone does, so there cannot be anything wrong about that." Good question. I will let the Word of God answer for you, so it will not just be my own thoughts and ideas. Then you cannot come to me and say that I am too extreme. As I have said before, there were some things I did two years ago that I do not do today. The reason is that God has been working with me and has led me into deeper holiness and purity. He wishes to do that for His whole church and come back one day for a pure bride, one who has kept herself unstained by the world.

Pure and undefiled religion in the sight of our God and Father is this: to visit orphans and widows in their distress, and to keep oneself unstained by the world. (James 1:27 NASB)

Higher standard

Another of the things I no longer practice today as I did before is going to the cinema and watching movies because, today, I know that I should not play with sin.

"It is not a sin to go to the cinema, is it?" No, it is not, and it is not a sin to have a TV, but it is sin if you fill yourself with the wrong stuff, if what you see is impure, or if it makes you live impurely. If you, for example, watch something sexual that creates a wrong desire in you, then it is sin. This is sometimes enough to cause the committing of fornication, and fornicators will not inherit the Kingdom of God. When you dream at night, it often relates to something you have seen or experienced in the last couple of days or even farther back. When I was watching TV and going to see movies, I would sometimes dream about something impure and sinful, which made me wake up with a bad conscience. It really annoyed me. I had remorse toward God, and my day was ruined. One day, I asked God why I could not control the things I dreamed about, and why I dreamed about something sinful. He said to me that it was because I lived in sin and filled myself with sinful things. I put my TV, movies, and other things away because I knew that the times I dreamed about something impure was almost always after I had seen something sinful on TV or in a movie. It is different today. I do not dream about wrong things anymore, and if something comes to my mind at night, I feel that I can control it. I know there are many who dream about impure things, and I just want to say to you that what you fill yourself with is often what you dream about at night. Therefore, if you dream about something impure, it is about time you started to give up some things and fill yourself with something else.

> In a dream, in a vision of the night, when deep sleep falls on men as they slumber in their beds, he may speak in their ears and terrify them with warnings, to turn man from wrongdoing ... (Job 33:15-17 NIV)

God's standard

It is proven that watching TV works in the same way as when one goes into a trance. You shut off the outside world and real life, and you open yourself to all the influences that come through the TV. Why do you think TV advertisements work so well? Because the influence goes right through. If you think you cannot be influenced because you are strong and can just turn it off when something wrong shows up, then you should think again. The opposite is proven.

The Bible clearly tells us that we should not watch and fill ourselves with something that is wrong. However, before we look at what God says through His Word, it is important, as I mentioned before, that you do not begin to imitate what others do. "But my parents can watch those movies, and they are serving God. And there was this person in the church who recommended this movie or this program." Remember that the anointing and power do not depend on whether you live purely or not. What if the person who recommended the movie he had seen later fell into sin because of it?

Do not just look at others, but look primarily at what God says is right and wrong. We have to look at God's standard for His people.

The big problem about TV is that sin slowly sneaks in, and your limits get pushed more and more. When I started to date my wife Lene, her limits were very sharp in relation to what was good to watch and what was not. I thought that she was pretty delicate and that she should relax a bit. However, as time went by, I realized that it was not her that had a problem. It was me. I was dull in distinguishing between good and evil. I was influenced so much by the world—and other Christians—that I did not admit that what I saw came directly from hell. Her discernment was sharp because she came from a family where they did not have a TV. This allowed her to see right away if something wrong came up. She could see what had a bad influence. Today, it is the same way with me. I cannot stand watching certain things I used to watch.

The Bible says that it is a sin to steal, murder, and fornicate. If we are completely honest, is this not what most people are filling them-selves with when they watch TV?

> *He who walks righteously and speaks uprightly, who despises gain from fraud and from oppression, who shakes his hand free from the taking of bribes, who stops his ears from hearing of bloodshed and shuts his eyes to avoid looking upon evil. (Isaiah 33:15 AMP)*

The Bible ranks the righteous one side by side with the one who stops his ears from hearing about bloodshed and shuts his eyes to avoid looking upon evil. This means that we, as righteous Christians, should not fill ourselves with murder, fornication, or other sinful things. How much is left to see on TV that does not show murder or sex? Not much, especially in movies. Most movies today contain sex and murder, and usually both. You can call me fanatical or whatever you want, but it is not me who made this up. It is the Word of God. If you want to be free from sin, then you must hate it and not pay to sit and fill yourself with it.

> *Therefore, since Christ suffered for us in the flesh, arm yourselves also with the same mind, for he who has suffered in the flesh has ceased from sin.* (1 Peter 4:1 NKJV)

We will now go further and look at what our relationship toward sin must be in our churches. There is something about sin in the churches that is a big problem today. Sin hinders the power of God from breaking through, and we as individuals should know that if we have sin in our lives, we will not see breakthrough in the church.

9

SIN IN THE CHURCH

Some time ago, I attended a meeting where someone shared a testimony. He mentioned that he had been to a service in another church where he received intercessory prayer. The preacher asked him if he had been smoking because he smelled of nicotine, which he admitted. Then the preacher told him that he should be happy it was not him who was the pastor in the church where he went because then he would be thrown out. After the testimony the man started to thank the leadership in his own church for being as they were and not throwing him out because of smoking.

When we heard this, my wife turned to me and asked if it was a compliment to the congregation. I thought that it was definitely not so. Quite the contrary! There is nothing to be thankful for if the attitude toward sin is so slack. Of course, you should not get thrown out just because you once smoked a cigarette, but there is something here that we have lost. The Bible gives us some clear statements regarding sin in the congregation, but we have become humanistic and secular in so many ways that we have deprived God's Word of power.

"But you cannot throw people out of the church just because they sin because that is not love." Is that true? What if one person in the church is living in conscious sin, and you know about it? Is it not the most loving thing that you can do to make the person aware of the problem? I do not mean that we should throw out all the people who fall into sin. We must speak with them, so they can repent. "But what if they do not admit that it is a problem and do not repent?" It should not be necessary to exclude people from the church, but we have fallen completely into the opposite ditch and are allowing too many things. If there is one in the congregation who lives in conscious sin, is it showing love if we allow it? What does it help if we allow sin when God does not? We can pretend that everything is all right, but if people are living in conscious sin, they are on their way to hell.

When people today are living in sin and will not repent, we do not exclude them from the congregation. Why? Is it because we want to be a big church? If they live in sin and will not repent, then it does not matter if they are members of a church or not. If you live in sin, you will not inherit the Kingdom of God.

"We wish to have many people in our church, so that is why we do not punish sin so hard. If we do, they will just find another church to go to." Is it not possible that one of the reasons for not having more members is that we allow something that God clearly forbids in His Word? Have we forgotten that we cannot lead people to God ourselves? They cannot come to God unless the Holy Spirit draws them (John 6:44). If we allow something that God clearly forbids, then it will hinder His Spirit from working as He could, and we will not see the breakthrough we long for.

Dangerous subject

I know I am touching a very dangerous subject here, but I believe God wants me to address this because it is a problem today.

When the Bible says that people should be excluded from the church for sin, we should not take it as a blanket statement that if someone sins, they must immediately be thrown out. We must judge in each case how to best deal with the person, since there can be various reasons for their sin. There might be, for example, a stronghold in someone's life that must be broken first before they can be set free.

Let us look closer at what God intended when speaking of sin in the congregation. Do not judge me and say that I am harsh and just want to throw this and that person out because that is not what I want. I have myself been in leadership of a church where there have been problems with sin. I once stood and talked to a girl who was walking farther and farther away from God. One of the reasons was that she got in with some "wrong" friends. One day, she visited my wife and me. We talked to her, but she was completely closed. I spoke harshly but in love, so she could understand that it was a serious problem, but she would not listen. When she left, I felt really grieved because I knew she was in danger of perishing. I questioned whether I had been too harsh with her. It was difficult for me, and it was not pleasant being in that position.

Some time later, after we moved to another city, I felt that if I had to be in leadership again one day, I wanted it confirmed to be 100% sure because of the great responsibility one has as a leader.

Do not think then that I treat lightly what I mention here. Today, I do not feel that I was too harsh with the girl because she will always know that there is something wrong as long as she is not living with God, and she will not forget what we told her. God now has something to work with in her. I could have chosen to be nice by saying: "What you are doing is not so good, but God is still with you, and we are still with you, so do not be sorry." I think that would have hindered her from seeing the seriousness of what she was doing. No matter how much we say that it is not so bad and everything will be fine, it does not change the fact that it is actually bad and that perhaps the person is on their way to hell.

I believe if we pay more attention to the consequences of sin in our churches, people will look at sin more seriously. It will make them think twice before they do something stupid. It is better to be rebuked while there is still time to turn it around, even if it does not feel nice. If you live in conscious sin, you will perish. It does not matter if you are a pastor or attend a church. Let's deal with the sin as long as there is time because one day it will be too late!

The Word of God is true

"Moreover if your brother sins against you, go and tell him his fault between you and him alone. If he hears you, you have gained your brother. But if he will not hear, take with you one or two more, that 'by the mouth of two or three witnesses every word may be established.' And if he refuses to hear them, tell it to the church. But if he refuses even to hear the church, let him be to you like a heathen and a tax collector." (Matthew 18:15-17 NKJV)

That passage shows that excluding people from the congregation is the last resort. Hopefully, it will never come that far. However, if we see a brother or sister sin, we should not be indifferent (1 John 5:16).

We should be attentive to one another. We should exhort and help one another, so that our brother or sister will not fall.

> *My brothers, if one of you should wander from the truth and someone should bring him back, remember this: Whoever turns a sinner from the error of his way will save him from death and cover over a multitude of sins.* (James 5:19-20 NIV)

When sin first comes into a person's life, it dims their ability to see the problem clearly. That's why it is important that we help one another. It really means so much when we step outside ourselves to help another.

> *Brothers, if someone is caught in a sin, you who are spiritual should restore him gently. But watch yourself, or you also may be tempted. Carry each other's burdens, and in this way you will fulfill the law of Christ.* (Galatians 6:1-2 NIV)

Later I will explain more about standing together and exhorting one another, but first we must look at something else:

> *It is actually reported that there is immorality among you, and immorality of such a kind as does not exist even among the Gentiles, that someone has his father's wife. You have become arrogant and have not mourned instead, so that the one who had done this deed would be removed from your midst. For I, on my part, though absent in body but present in spirit, have already judged him who has so committed this, as though I were present. In the name of our Lord Jesus, when you are assembled, and I with you in spirit, with the power of our Lord Jesus, I have decided to deliver such a one to Satan for the destruction of his flesh, so that his spirit may be saved in the day of the Lord Jesus. Your boasting is not good. Do you not know that a little leaven leavens the whole lump of dough? Clean out the old leaven so that you may be a new lump, just as you are in fact unleavened. For Christ our Passover also has been sacrificed. Therefore let us celebrate the feast, not with old leaven, nor with the leaven of malice and wickedness, but with the unleavened bread of sincerity and truth. I wrote you in my letter not to associate with immoral people; I did not at all mean with the immoral people of this*

*world, or with the covetous and swindlers, or with idolaters, for then
you would have to go out of the world. But actually, I wrote to you
not to associate with any so-called brother if he is an immoral person,
or covetous, or an idolater, or a reviler, or a drunkard, or a swindler—
not even to eat with such a one. For what have I to do with judging
outsiders? Do you not judge those who are within the church? But
those who are outside, God judges. REMOVE THE WICKED MAN
FROM AMONG YOURSELVES.* (1 Corinthians 5:1-13 NASB)

These are intense words, that the man who committed fornication
must be delivered to Satan. But let us look deeper. When God comes
with this commandment, it is not because He does not want the man
to come back to Him. No, God wants all people to get saved. He does
not want anyone to perish, and as we see in verse five, the reason for
excluding him from the congregation is "for the destruction of his flesh,
so that his spirit may be saved in the day of the Lord Jesus." Even if we
think it was not a loving act to "deliver someone to Satan," it is actually
done with a loving end in mind—that no one should perish. The reason
sin has such great consequence is so the sinner will realize how big a
problem sin is and cause them to repent and come back to God. It is
important that we begin to be obedient toward God and not think that
we know what is best because God is far greater than us.

It is easier said than done when you have to speak to someone who
is living in sin and perhaps exclude them from the church. After all, it
is humans we are dealing with. Nobody wants to do something wrong.
As I said before, I have been in leadership in a church where we had to
deal with one who did not want to realize that sin was a problem. It
requires wisdom, but what God wants from us is obedience, even if it
sometimes may be uncomfortable.

A little leaven

When Paul says that "a little leaven leavens the whole lump of
dough," then there is nothing else to do than to be obedient toward
God's Word. God is a holy God, and He cannot have anything to do
with sin.

That is why it is important that we do not tolerate sin in our
churches. We all have a desire to see a breakthrough, people getting

saved, and people getting healed and set free. This is not something we can accomplish by ourselves. Only God can do it. No matter how much we try to see it happen in our churches, we cannot do it ourselves. Only the power of God can do it. I believe there is a connection between not seeing the power of God moving, as we wish to see it, and allowing sin in our churches. Since we do not see much of God's power in our churches, we are trying to make people come in many different ways. We try to reach them by worldly means; for example, with video-marathons and disco-parties. Youth meetings are about having fun, playing games, and watching movies instead of being about the power of God. It is because we have become so desperate to reach them. Instead of repenting and crying out to God, we let "the world" come into our churches. We try to compete with "the world" so that we can reach people in this manner. However, people do not need us to become like "the world." They need to see God.

If we act based on the worry that some of the members of the church will leave and go to another church, then we are saying in essence that it is all right to drink alcohol, smoke, party, etc., and the purity, holiness, and radicalism that God wants disappear. Maybe someone you have been praying for finally gets saved and comes to church. There, they experience the same things they saw in the world but to a lesser degree. They begin to think they might just as well live in the world, since it is more wild and more fun, and they are gone.

Do not eat with everyone

... I wrote to you not to associate with any so-called brother if he is an immoral person, or covetous, or an idolater, or a reviler, or a drunkard, or a swindler—not even to eat with such a one. (1 Corinthians 5:11 NASB)

If a brother or sister starts to live sinfully, we often handle it in a completely wrong way. Instead of showing them how serious their sin is by giving them a choice between their sin or the fellowship in the church, we compromise and lead them to believe that it is not so bad. Perhaps we say it is not so good, for example, that the person concerned moved in with his or her girlfriend or boyfriend, but there are really no consequences in the church. If we eat with them and have fun with them like before, then they will not see the seriousness of living in sin.

If, for example, my best friend considered taking drugs, I would do everything possible to talk him out of it. I would try to make him understand that it was the most stupid thing he could do, and, in this way, he would be warned. If he still did not want to listen, I would try to save him by giving our friendship a test. I would tell him that, if he wanted to take drugs, we could not be friends any longer. I would hope that by setting that boundary, it would make him consider it one more time. Then he could see at least one of the consequences right here and right now, and the choice he was going to make would change from being a choice between taking drugs and avoiding making me mad, to a choice between drugs and our friendship. If he still chose the drugs, I would tell him that if he turned around, I would be there as a friend again, but, in the meantime, I would not have anything to do with him.

I hope everyone can see from the perspective of this example that what I am doing is not so stupid, and that it exactly shows that I care about him. This is the same thing that Paul is talking about. It is not because one does not want to have anything to do with the person living in sin. It is to save them. Think about this the next time you stand in a situation like this, and pray that God may show you what you have to do. In this way, we avoid following our own humanistic and worldly way of thinking and, instead, start doing what is best for the person concerned in the long run.

Remove the wicked man from among yourselves

The Word says that we should remove the wicked man from among ourselves (1 Corinthians 5:13). Removing the wicked is important for two reasons—the person who is living in sin will experience its consequence so that he might repent, and conscious sin in our congregations will affect the whole church and not just the sinner. Sin hinders, among other things, the Holy Spirit from moving as He wants.

To understand this, we will look closer at Achan from the Old Testament. You can read in Joshua 6 about the Israelites preparing to take Jericho. God gave the command that they should abstain from taking the accursed things, lest they should become accursed when they take them. *"But all the silver and gold, and vessels of bronze and iron, are consecrated to the Lord; they shall come into the treasury of the Lord"* (Joshua 6: 19).

Let's recap this event thinking of Israel as "the church." God had issued a command for the whole church, but one man named Achan took some of the accursed things that were under the ban and hid them in his tent so that no one could see them. The consequence of Achan's action was that God did not go with them the next time they were going to war. This was a very easy opponent, and only 2,000 or 3,000 men were needed. What happened, however, was that thirty-six men died, the rest fled, and the whole church lost their courage.

Then Joshua cried out to God and asked why He had failed them:

So the LORD said to Joshua, "Rise up! Why is it that you have fallen on your face? Israel has sinned, and they have also transgressed My covenant which I commanded them. And they have even taken some of the things under the ban and have both stolen and deceived. Moreover, they have also put them among their own things. Therefore the sons of Israel cannot stand before their enemies; they turn their backs before their enemies, for they have become accursed. I will not be with you anymore unless you destroy the things under the ban from your midst." (Joshua 7:10-12 NASB)

Even though it was only one man, Achan, who had sinned, all of the Israelites were held responsible. The punishment did not fall just on Achan but on the whole congregation, and thirty-six men were killed as a result. The story continues with Achan, his children, animals, and everything he owned being stoned and burned. After they removed the wicked man from among themselves, they were able to easily prevail over those who had defeated them before. Why? Because this time God was with them (Joshua 6:18, Joshua 7-8, and Joshua 22:20).

This is a serious story, and together with what we have read from the New Testament, we see that sin in the congregation is not something to play with. That is another reason for standing together and helping one another, so that sin will not have a right to get into our lives and churches. In the next chapter, I will say more about the principle of standing together and exhorting one another.

10

LET US STAND TOGETHER

… but exhort one another daily, while it is called "Today," lest any
of you be hardened through the deceitfulness of sin.
(Hebrews 3:13 NKJV)

We all need one or more people who will stand together with us. We need someone who is not afraid of telling us the truth if we are about to do something stupid or have sin in our life. The Bible talks a lot about exhorting and helping one another, and even rebuking if sin is seen in the life of a brother or sister. It is important that we do this. It is rare that someone can or will acknowledge sin in his or her own life. Sin often sneaks in slowly, unnoticed, and that is why at times it is realized very late, maybe too late. Let us therefore speak the truth, in love, to one another without concealing anything.

It is said that love makes us blind. Sin also makes us blind. When sin is already at work in us, it is difficult for us to see it. The problem can not be seen anymore because the consciousness has been dazzled by it. In such cases, it is important to have someone who can tell you the truth, someone who can help you see the deception of sin and become free from it. It must be someone who can stand with you when you feel that Satan has come for a visit, and you experience an intense battle. You both can resist Satan's temptations together. Remember, there is exponential power when two stand together. And if there is sin in your life, then it is also important that you have someone you can confess it to because the only way to defeat sin is by letting it come out into the light.

But if we walk in the light as He is in the light, we have fellowship with one another, and the blood of Jesus Christ His Son cleanses us from all sin. (1 John 1:7 NKJV)

In the light

As long as the sin is in darkness, God cannot work with it. That is why it must come out into the light by being confessed to someone. You need to have a friend with whom you can be open, one who will not start laughing at you but understands how to keep a secret. One you can share everything with.

Unfortunately, these kinds of friends are rare, and we must be careful in our choices. It starts with slowly opening oneself and, in doing so, building a confidential friendship. Some time ago, I heard a friend say that one day he experienced a huge temptation relating to pornography. He hurried to call someone to come to him and stand together with him as he fought the attack. The person came, and they fought together to resist that temptation in Jesus' name and won. Most people would have probably kept the temptation to themselves so it would not come out into the light, which almost always results in succumbing to the temptation.

But each one is tempted when he is drawn away by his own desires and enticed. Then, when desire has conceived, it gives birth to sin; and sin, when it is full-grown, brings forth death. (James 1:14 NKJV)

Remember, as I have stated before, that there is always a way out of the temptations so that you do not have to give in. What my friend did by calling someone and confessing the temptation and bringing it out into the light is the only right thing to do if one wants to gain victory over sin.

The way he opened himself and said that he had experienced a battle helped me to know that if I need someone to stand with me, I can go to him. Why? Because I know that he will not laugh at me since he has experienced battles himself. We will all face battles.

It is important not to think you must be the only one going through temptations and battles because you are not. There is no reason for you to be embarrassed or think that you are weak, and fear what might happen if you mention your problem to someone. You should rather think about what might happen if you do not tell it to somebody. Remember that the only way to overcome sin is by living in the light, bringing everything into the light. Sin will eventually come out. Is it not better that it comes out now before it is too late? Remember that God sees everything, both when you are tempted and when you sin. Thinking that it is best to hide it to keep someone from thinking this or that is a deception straight from hell. As long as the sin is hidden, Satan has the power, but as soon as it comes out into the light, he cannot win. That is why it is so important that we open ourselves to one another when we experience a problem and not just when we experience victory.

> *Therefore confess your sins to each other and pray for each other so that you may be healed. The prayer of a righteous man is powerful and effective.* (James 5:16 NIV)

If you do not have anyone you can go to, work on finding someone you know you can trust and speak with him or her. Start to open yourself up. If you have friends who influence you in a bad direction, get new friends. Do not spend time with them. You are exceedingly influenced by those you spend time with. You become like those you socialize with. Therefore, find someone you would like to resemble in the way they live their life with God.

> *As iron sharpens iron, so one man sharpens another.* (Proverbs 27:17 NIV)

Face to face

I used to meet someone every week, and we talked together and prayed for each other. We took a piece of paper with twenty to thirty questions and asked each other the questions. In this way, it was much easier to talk about the more "private" areas in our lives. Some of the questions were: "Have you hurt someone with your words, either behind the person's back or face to face? Have you given in to temptation in sexual issues? Have you had romantic fantasies about someone other than your spouse, or have you read or seen sexually stimulating materials? Have you been under the influence of hash, alcohol, or similar?" It may seem a bit stiff to ask each other questions from a piece of paper, but thanks to that, it quickly became normal for us to talk about the more private issues that otherwise would have taken longer to dare to talk about.

Another good thing when meeting a person regularly is that if, for example, you are facing a temptation, then you know that you will soon have to stand face to face with someone and be asked if you have done this and that and then you will have to tell the truth. This makes you consider things one more time. As Christians, we cannot lie because liars do not belong to the Kingdom of God.

There should be so much fear of the Lord in one's life that it is not necessary for another person to be involved in order for one to consider his actions when facing temptation. God sees everything, including when we sin. If we sin, then that will have a consequence, no matter if others see it or not. However, being responsible before another person can help, so that we will see the consequence immediately. It can help us grow and learn to deal with the temptations. Let us therefore begin to open ourselves toward one another. It is better to become a little embarrassed than to perish. Remember that sin separates us from God. Let us begin to exhort one another, as Paul did, so we will not fall.

Dear friends, I urge you, as aliens and strangers in the world, to abstain from sinful desires, which war against your soul. (1 Peter 2:11 NIV)

What has happened?

I will continue with a small testimony of how we need one another:

When I first came to Jesus in 1995, I was an apprentice in a baker's shop. After I had been a Christian for three or four months, I was about to go back to the technical school for ten weeks together with some other guys I had been to school with earlier. There were three or four guys I hung out with a lot, and usually, when we were in school together, there was partying and boozing for all the ten weeks. We used to be those who had to try everything, but now it was a little different because

I had become a Christian. I felt that all of them should receive Jesus and start to believe. I had to take the train early in the morning, and while I was on the train, I was praying and felt really excited. I arrived at the school, and my old friends came to me: "What's up, Torben? Here we are again. How are you doing? Shall we go clubbing on Wednesday? There is cheap keg beer." Suddenly, I felt very small, and I did not have much to say.

Neither did I say a word the next day about having become a Christian. I felt that it was becoming harder and harder for me to resist the temptations that were there. Wednesday came, and my friends asked if I wanted to go clubbing. Even though I had decided at home that I would not go and would tell them that I had become a Christian, to my own surprise, I heard myself say: "No, I cannot go today, but maybe tomorrow." When I went home later, I felt completely wrecked, and everything with Jesus was suddenly so difficult.

What should I do? I knew deep down inside that they needed Jesus and that it would not be good if I went clubbing. Luckily, I did the right thing. I needed someone who could stand with me. I picked up the phone and called my cell group leader, but he could not come. After a moment of panic, I called my youth leader and told him that I was experiencing a battle and felt very confused. He said he would arrive in an hour, so I began to tidy up a bit. I was still very confused and dismayed, but when I was taking the trash out, I met two ladies from the church. They asked how I was doing, and I told them about the situation. They said right away that I should stand firm, and that God was with me, and so on. After a few minutes with them, the trash still in my hand, I was totally changed. I felt already that I had won. Some time later, when my youth leader arrived, I was really happy, and we talked a little and prayed together. When I arrived at the school the next day and the friends came to me and asked if I was going to the club with them that night, I said: "No, I don't want to go clubbing because I have met Jesus, and He has changed my life. You also need to meet Him." Then there was victory. After I said that I had become a Christian, there was no problem in resisting their offer. Two weeks later, someone from my class came and asked me what had happened with me since I did not want to go clubbing anymore. We had a really good conversation, and a week later, she met Jesus herself. What would have happened if I had not called and met those ladies from the church? I do not know, but it would definitely have ended differently. You see, we all need one another. We all have something to give, and when we stand together, Satan cannot come in and beat us.

Upbringing hurts

Let us not be afraid of rebuking one another if we see something wrong. Let us say it. I know it might not be the easiest thing to do, and it is not pleasant to be rebuked either, but it is so necessary. For example, if I start to talk about someone behind their back or do other wrong things, then my wife will surely tell me about it. What usually happens then is that I get a little annoyed at her. Why? Not because she is not right, but because it hurts. My flesh does not like it. After a few minutes, I have to admit that she is right, and I repent. It is not always so nice to be rebuked, but it is necessary if we are to reach the goal. Let us not be afraid to tell the truth if there is sin in somebody's life. That is the only loving and right thing to do.

> *Our fathers disciplined us for a little while as they thought best; but God disciplines us for our good, that we may share in his holiness. No discipline seems pleasant at the time, but painful. Later on, however, it produces a harvest of righteousness and peace for those who have been trained by it.* (Hebrews 12:10-11 NIV)

> *And we urge you, brothers, warn those who are idle, encourage the timid, help the weak, be patient with everyone. Make sure that nobody pays back wrong for wrong, but always try to be kind to each other and to everyone else.* (1 Thessalonians 5:14-15 NIV)

> *Brothers, if someone is caught in a sin, you who are spiritual should restore him gently. But watch yourself, or you also may be tempted. Carry each other's burdens, and in this way you will fulfill the law of Christ.* (Galatians 6:1-2 NIV)

11

NOW WHAT?

We have looked a bit at sound doctrine and the fear of the Lord, as well as grace and sin in the church and in our own lives. Now what? Well, I hope that God has spoken to you through what we have covered, that you have received a revelation of a new side of sin and what it does in our lives, and that you will get to experience more fear of the Lord than you have had before. I will then say as Paul:

> ... *exercise yourself toward godliness. For bodily exercise profits a little, but godliness is profitable for all things, having promise of the life that now is and of that which is to come.* (1 Timothy 4:7-8 NKJV)

I can boldly say I feel that through this book, God has called me to lead His church into holiness and godliness, which will allow us to see His power as never before. God has revealed to me much of the teaching here through an extended period of time in sanctification and prayer. I can boldly say that this is a prophetic book. My prayer is that it will help us as Christians to deal with the sin in our lives—as individuals and in our churches. I am certain that sin is a huge obstacle to seeing the breakthroughs we pray and beg for. The way forward is through prayer. I am convinced that in the time to come, we will see a breakthrough in connection to prayer because we are about to realize that we can only win this battle we are in with spiritual weaponry, which is prayer.

"Then why do you not just write about prayer?" you may ask. It is because we must understand that before we can experience major victories through prayer, we have to be living a pure and holy life in repentance. If there is sin in our lives, God does not hear us.

> *Surely the arm of the LORD is not too short to save, nor his ear too dull to hear. But your iniquities have separated you from your God; your sins have hidden his face from you, so that he will not hear.* (Isaiah 59:1-2 NIV)

Many prayers have been prayed through many years, but I think we can pray from now on until Jesus comes again without seeing the revival that we yearn for as long as we allow sin in our lives and churches. I am also convinced that if we, as the church, come back to sound doctrine so that we have the true fear of the Lord in our lives and churches and deal with sin, then we will start to see God's power as never before. We will start to see sinners have a desire to get out of sin and repent, and people will be set free and healed.

God speaks to His church

Some time ago, a prophecy was read at a meeting I had attended. One person in the church had received this prophecy and written it down. As I write it here now, I believe it is a prophetic word from God, not to a certain church but to God's people.

"The Lord says to the church:

I desire a people with pure hearts. I am tired of getting honor only from your lips, and not your hearts. I am a holy and jealous God, who cannot stand sin. I sent My Son to the earth, so that you can receive forgiveness for your trespasses, but you are playing with My grace. When you know a sin is in your life, I want you to carry it to the cross and leave it there. It is not about whether you feel that you are ready to do this and that. When My Holy Spirit moves in your hearts, then you MUST obey. It is a decision I want you to make if you desire holiness in your lives.

I wish to reach out to the whole world with my love and salvation, but you are in the way. I cannot come through with my Holy Spirit. You are not worthy to carry my glory and holiness out to the world because your hearts are filled with sin that is not dealt with. Do you think I sent the most precious I have to this earth for fun and let Him suffer so much under your sin that I had to leave Him in the moment of death? NO! I did it out of love, and it hurts Me so much when you take it so lightly. I cannot stand it. If you take your commitment to Me seriously, if you treat your life in eternity seriously, THEN REPENT!!!

Oh, My children, do not harden your hearts when I speak to you by My Holy Spirit and remind you of things. Make a choice and deal with it. It will hurt in your flesh, and you will feel humiliated and displayed toward people. You will experience Satan's attack and his attempt to make you stop, BUT DO IT! Today rather than tomorrow. He has no right to speak into your lives when you belong to Me!!!

I long so unspeakably much to be allowed to permeate your lives. I desire to see My love and holiness through you shining out to this world. THE WORLD NEEDS YOU. You are My messengers, I do not have any other!!! Oh, how I long for you to surrender EVERYTHING to Me, so that I might be allowed to bless you and let you be part of the revival I am expecting to send over your country and your cities. You have had many words from Me about revival, and you do not believe it anymore. You do not pray for it anymore. No, because you have hardened yourselves! The revival is here, but I am missing workers who will lay everything down for Me to live a life that is holy and well pleasing to Me.

You hypocrites, you look at the outward things. I cannot use your traditions and rituals for anything. If you are not surrendered to Me, then it is empty words and actions and even mockery toward My holiness. You have many skills. I have given them to you, but not to walk in your own power. I am led when I see it. You cannot accomplish anything if it is not Me ... If you will choose to repent from your sin, then you will see My glory break through and a revival rise over your city, yes, even the whole country, but if you will not, then you have hardened yourselves and defied My commandments. You are no longer My servants, merely hearers of the Word and not its doers. Oh, how I cry, when I look at your hearts. If you would just let go of all your own and let Me come through, I have so much to give you. It is not Me who holds back, but you who are in the way so that I cannot pour it out. Repent today. Repent!

These are harsh words. It is something we should read again and again and really take it to ourselves. When He points at something in our lives, we must obey and repent, so God can come through. This prophetic word confirms much of the content in this book. God is a holy God who hates sin. We should not play with His grace. God wishes to transform our nations, but if we allow sin and live a lukewarm life, He cannot use us. Let us not be a hindrance to God's kingdom breaking through by failing to repent. Let us meditate on it and let God speak to us. Let us live a life in surrender and fear of the Lord where we humble ourselves before Him. When we live a surrendered life in fear of the Lord and call out to Him with the full force of our being, we will get to see an outpouring of the Spirit as never before.

> *And it shall come to pass afterward, that I will pour out my spirit upon all flesh; and your sons and your daughters shall prophesy, your old men shall dream dreams, your young men shall see visions: And also upon the servants and upon the handmaids in those days will I pour out my spirit.* (Joel 2:28-29 KJV)

When we read about this pouring out, which we also saw at Pentecost, we can see that verse one begins with: "And it shall come to pass afterward." When it says that it shall come to pass *afterward*, then it means that something happened *before* what we have just read, something that had a meaning for this pouring out:

> *Therefore also now, saith the LORD, turn ye even to me with all your heart, and with fasting, and with weeping, and with mourning: And rend your heart, and not your garments, and turn unto the LORD your God: for he is gracious and merciful, slow to anger, and of great kindness, and repenteth him of the evil.* (Joel 2:12-13 KJV)

You can read here that God urges them to repent. He urges them to turn with all their heart and cleanse themselves from sin. Then after they have repented for their sin, verse 15 says that they call together for prayer. First repentance, then prayer, and then comes the result in verse 18:

Then the LORD will be jealous for His land, and pity His people. (Joel 2:18 KJV)

Let us not be a hindrance

We need God to spare our nations. In many ways are we living in a world that is worse than Sodom and Gomorrah. God desires to see our countries transformed. Let us not be a hindrance to God by allowing sin. We have deceived ourselves much too long by believing that we can live as we wish and then still pray to Him and expect that He hears us. Many prayers have been prayed for our countries, but we have not seen a breakthrough. Why? Because the conditions are not all met. I believe with all my heart that if we as His church step into what, among other things, I have mentioned in this book about living a pure life in the fear of the Lord, and start to preach the Word as it really is, then we will see a revival like never before. We must preach that sin separates us from God and that repentance from sin gains admission to Him through Jesus. Before we continue to cry out to God for revival, let us deal with sin, and then we will begin to see our countries transformed.

He who turns away his ear from listening to the law, even his prayer is an abomination. (Proverbs 28:9 NASB)

However, there is hope because *"The prayer of a righteous man is powerful and effective"* (James 5:16 NIV).

The end

May God bless you in your life with Him. May you step into the life that God has for you. May we all be sanctified, so we who are living with Jesus now and telling others about Him may not perish but obtain eternal life.

But I discipline my body and bring it into subjection, lest, when I have preached to others, I myself should become disqualified. (1 Corinthians 9:27 NKJV)

But now having been set free from sin, and having become slaves of God, you have your fruit to holiness, and the end, everlasting life. (Romans 6:22 NKJV)

And may we all bear the fruits that repentance requires, so we can be well-pleasing to God.

Then he said to the multitudes that came out to be baptized by him, "Brood of vipers! Who warned you to flee from the wrath to come? Therefore bear fruits worthy of repentance, and do not begin to say to yourselves: [I attend church. I read the Bible and pray to God. I witness to people. I speak in tongues, and so on.] 'We have Abraham as our father.' For I say to you that God is able to raise up children to Abraham from these stones. And even now the ax is laid to the root of the trees. Therefore every tree which does not bear good fruit is cut down and thrown into the fire. (Luke 3:7-9 NKJV) [Bracketed words added]

First to those in Damascus, then to those in Jerusalem and in all Judea, and to the Gentiles also, I preached that they should repent and turn to God and prove their repentance by their deeds. (Acts 26:20 NIV) .

Three Years Later

By getting a revelation of "Sound Doctrine" and having my eyes opened to the fact that God is really holy and that He will judge sin and disobedience where it can be found, I have experienced freedom that is still the same after three years. I still feel this freedom from sin and boldness toward God that I did not have before. My whole life has been changed by what happened three years ago.

By the revelation of "Sound Doctrine," I have a deeper understanding of the whole Word of God. Others have experienced the same when they heard the message of this book. Today, I do not have to skip the places in the Bible where it speaks of "sin against the Holy Spirit," "sin leading to death" (1 John 5:16), and where Jesus says that if the salt loses its power, it will never become salt again (Matthew 5:13), and so on. All of this is connected, and it makes sense.

As an ending to this book, I will tell you more about what it means to lose your salvation, sin against the Holy Spirit, and how to get to know the truth. Remember, as I have said throughout, there is a difference between committing a sin and continually living in conscious, willful sin. If this creates a wrong form of fear in you, which I have also mentioned before, then go back and read the book from the beginning, so that you will get the right understanding of it.

This teaching should cause you to see a need to surrender everything to God and live in the light, which happened in me. I understood that I could not have a bit of the world and a bit of God, but that it was either one or the other. I understood that I should not treat my salvation lightly, but that it has been something I should work on with fear and trembling, as Paul says it in Philippians 2:12. I understood that ten minutes in prayer to God here and there, while I am filling myself with a lot of other stuff, is not enough. It is really a question of dying to yourself and your own desires and of understanding that we do not live for ourselves, but that we let Jesus be Lord in our lives in all areas (Galatians 2:20). We really need to live in a close relationship with God, seek Him, get to know Him, and free ourselves from sin, so we can endure the race ahead of us.

The Bible says that sound doctrine creates true fear of the Lord. Therefore, if this fear of the Lord is missing in our churches, it must be a sign that we do not preach the true Word of God and sound doctrine, but just the things that tickle people's itching ears, as Paul warns us:

> *For the time will come when men will not put up with sound doctrine. Instead, to suit their own desires, they will gather around them a great number of teachers to say what their itching ears want to hear. They will turn their ears away from the truth and turn aside to myths.* (2 Timothy 4:3-4 NIV)

First Timothy 2:4 says that: "(God) wants all men to be saved and to come to the knowledge of the truth." We must understand that there are depths to grasp. Some things will not come when we raise our hands during a service but by the revelation of God and His Word. Jesus says that we shall get to know the truth, and the knowledge of the truth shall make us free. It happens when we keep His Word and acknowledge Him.

> *To the Jews who had believed him, Jesus said, "If you hold to my teaching, you are really my disciples. Then you will know the truth, and the truth will set you free."* (John 8:31-32 NIV)

Many who attend church today live in sin, and one of the reasons for this is that they have never really learned the truth. Through the knowledge of the truth, you will realize that it is a holy and righteous God that we serve. Through the knowledge of the truth, you will see sin as sin and understand what it means that sin has a consequence in your life. Through the knowledge of the truth, you will get true fear of the Lord. When you get this fear of the Lord and have the right attitude to keep away from sin, God frees you from temptations, and it gets easier to overcome sin. However, if you are living in filthy lust and not listening to the Lord's rebukes, God will allow you to remain in sin until the Judgment Day.

Sin is not to be played with. When the presence of God was so strongly present during the incident with Ananias and Sapphira lying to the Holy Spirit (Acts 5), the result was that they both fell dead right there. After that incident, the whole church and everyone who heard about it were filled with great fear and experienced even more progress.

If we have really received the knowledge of the truth and repented, got baptized in water, and experienced the baptism in the Holy Spirit and freedom from sin, and then keep sinning continuously, knowing full well what consequences it brings, the same thing that happened to Ananias and Sapphira can happen.

> If we deliberately keep on sinning after we have received the knowledge of the truth, no sacrifice for sins is left, but only a fearful expectation of judgment and of raging fire that will consume the enemies of God. Anyone who rejected the law of Moses died without mercy on the testimony of two or three witnesses. How much more severely do you think a man deserves to be punished who has trampled the Son of God under foot, who has treated as an unholy thing the blood of the covenant that sanctified him, and who has insulted the Spirit of grace? (Hebrews 10:26-29 NIV)

Since one of the tasks of the Holy Spirit is to convince the world about sin, some think that sinning against the Holy Spirit is not to believe in Jesus. However, this Scripture indicates that it is more than that. If it talks about someone who does not believe in Jesus and does not care about the truth, then he does not walk around with a fearful expectation of the judgment since he does not believe that there will be a judgment. This Scripture says that we can come so far away that there is no forgiveness anymore, even if we later would like to get it, because we have sinned against the Holy Spirit.

This should make us as Christians realize that we must treat seriously our salvation and what Jesus did on the cross. We have to see the need to live close to God and make sure that the wrong things do not come into our lives and, as a result, hinder us from reaching the goal—the salvation of our soul. Therefore, we must make sure that we keep ourselves on fire throughout our whole life and not let the deception of sin fool us.

I hope that through this teaching, people will get to know the truth, which will set them free. The problem with receiving this kind of teaching is that we often take our own experience and put it above the Word of God. We think: "It is not like that because I know someone who lived with God for many years, who later fell completely away from God and lived in conscious sin, and, after that, came back to God again." To this I want to say that the Word of God is evident:

> *It is impossible for those who have once been enlightened, who have tasted the heavenly gift, who have shared in the Holy Spirit, who have tasted the goodness of the word of God and the powers of the coming age, if they fall away, to be brought back to repentance, because to their loss they are crucifying the Son of God all over again and subjecting him to public disgrace.* (Hebrews 6:4-6 NIV)

Many who attend churches today have not really come to the knowledge of the truth, and many are still living in deception. They may have tasted God a little bit, but they are not really saved. They may have had an experience or a touch from God, but they have never really repented or laid their lives down to live with Jesus as their Lord and Savior.

When we speak about receiving forgiveness, we must remember that forgiveness and repentance are interconnected.

Charles Finney, one of the world's greatest evangelists, came up with a good definition of what true repentance and penitence are. From the book, *Principles for Revival*, he teaches how to lead a sinner to God.

"Penitence always involves hate toward sin. It is feeling about sin the same way as God does. It always involves renunciation of sin. Get sinners to understand this! Penitent sinners do not feel the same way as the non-penitent sinners think they do. The non-penitent sinners think that if they become Christians, they will have to stay away from parties, theatre, games, and other things they care about. They think that they can never have fun again if they have to stop with these things. But that is far from the truth. Christianity does not make them unhappy by excluding them from enjoyable things because the first step of becoming a Christian is to repent, to change your mind about all these things. They do not seem to understand that a repentant person does not have any desire after these things; they have abandoned them and turned their hearts from them. Sinners feel that they would like to go to sinful places and make sinful things in the same manner as they do now. Living as a Christian, they feel, will become a long, unhappy sacrifice. This is a misunderstanding."

And then Finney makes this radical statement:

"I know some people who claim to be Christians who would enjoy going back to their old lifestyle if they did not have to fear for their reputation. But listen: If they feel this way, they cannot claim to be Christians; they do not hate sin. If they long for their old lifestyle, they are showing that they have never really repented because repentance always consists in changing points of view and feelings. If they had truly repented, they would have turned with disgust from these things instead of wanting them. Instead of longing for Egypt and wishing to go back to their old friends and companionships, they would find their greatest pleasure in obeying God." (*Principles for Revival*, page 280)

I believe if one really gets through what we are reading here, they will not backslide again. They will want to do as Peter said:

... *"Lord, to whom shall we go? You have the words of eternal life."* (John 6:68 NIV)

You will put your hand to the plough without looking back, and then you will be fit for the Kingdom of God.

But Jesus said to him, "No one, having put his hand to the plow, and looking back, is fit for the Kingdom of God." (Luke 9:62 NKJV)

Then David said to Nathan, "I have sinned against the LORD." (2 Sam. 12:13 NAS)

King David was a man who lived in repentance and confessed his sin. That is why he was a man after God's heart.

Ananias and Sapphira committed a sin that was much smaller in their eyes, but God's judgment fell upon them immediately (Acts 5). Their attitude toward sin was completely different from what it should have been. They had the Holy Spirit in them, but they treated their sin much too lightly anyway.

Just like David, we must quickly fall down at God's feet and ask for forgiveness. We must fear God, as I have encouraged in this book. Then God's grace will be as we read about in Psalm 103:

For as the heavens are high above the earth, so great is His mercy toward those who fear Him. (Psalm 103:11 NKJV)

This is sound doctrine, the doctrine that creates true fear of the Lord, as you perhaps already can perceive.

God bless you,

Torben Søndergaard
www.TheLastReformation.com

Christian, Disciple, or Slave

What is a Christian? The answer to this essential question today unfortunately depends on who you ask. In this book, you get the biblical answer to what a Christian really is, and how you can become a Christian. You will also be taken on a journey through the Bible as we look at various words people use for those who follow Jesus, words such as "Christian," "disciple," and "slave."

Many of us have heard the expression: "I am a Christian, but in my own way," or "I'm a Christian, but I'm not so much into it." But, is it even possible to be a Christian in one's own personal way? The author argues that, according to the Bible, the answer is no, just as it is not possible to be a disciple or a slave in one's own personal way.

The book is written for both Christian and non-Christian. A radical book, it takes a hard look at what Jesus Himself said about being a Christian. Jesus' words are extremely radical, but it is the place where we get the true answer to the question: "What is a real Christian?"

COMING OCTOBER 2013
This book may be purchased in paperback from
USA: www.TheLaurusCompany.com/store and Amazon.com
Outside the USA: Amazon.ca, .co.uk, .de, .at, .fr, .it, .es
and other retailers around the world.
Also available in eBook format for e-readers from their respective stores.

The Last Reformation

Back to the New Testament model of Discipleship

Much of what we see expressed in the church today is built on more than just the New Testament. It's built, instead, mostly on the Old Testament, Church culture, and Paganism. It is therefore imperative that we as God's people dare to stop and take a closer look at the Church today and compare it to the first Church we read about in the Bible. If we are to succeed in making disciples of all nations then we must go back to the "template" we find in the Bible.

Let the reformation begin!

Most of us as Christians have inherited a way of being church and being disciples. Torben challenges us to question this by using examples from the Bible and from Church history. This book is challenging and sharp, but we all want to see more people believing in Jesus, disciples trained, and churches growing stronger and multiplying. This is why we believe **The Last Reformation** *is important for our thinking about how we want to be and do church in our times.*

• From the Foreword by Charles Kridiotis and Mattias Nordenberg

This book may be purchased in paperback from
USA: www.TheLaurusCompany.com/store and Amazon.com
Outside the USA: Amazon.ca, .co.uk, .de, .at, .fr, .it, .es
and other retailers around the world.
Also available in eBook format for e-readers from their respective stores.

"Life as a Christian"

"Complete the Race"

"Deceived?" (Booklet)

"The Twisted Race" (Booklet

These Publications can be found on the author's website at:

www.TheLastReformation.com

ABOUT THE AUTHOR

Torben Søndergaard

Torben Søndergaard lives in Denmark in the city of Herning with his wife, Lene, and their three children.

Torben grew up in a non-Christian family. On April 5, 1995, after attending a church service with a friend, he turned to God and had a strong, personal encounter with Jesus that totally changed his life. Five years later, from a Scripture in the Bible and in a sort of desperation after more of God, Torben started on a 40-day fast that transformed many things in his life. His eyes were more open to God's Word and what the gospel is about. He began to understand how lukewarm and far away from the truth Christians had become. He saw that God had called him to speak His Word without compromise.

Torben has worked as an evangelist and church planter for some years. Today, he is having meetings around Denmark and abroad, where he sees many people getting healed and set free. He is the author of six other books, has been on both radio and TV many times. Apart from that, he is the founder of the websites: OplevJesus.dk, Mission.dk, and the English websites:

TheLastReformation.com and TheLastReformationUSA.com

SKINS

A-Z

KATE MOLLOY

JOHN BLAKE

Published by John Blake Publishing Ltd,
3 Bramber Court, 2 Bramber Road,
London W14 9PB, England

www.johnblakepublishing.co.uk

www.facebook.com/Johnblakepub   facebook

twitter.com/johnblakepub   twitter

First published in paperback in 2012

ISBN: 978-1-84358-392-9

British Library Cataloguing-in-Publication Data:

A catalogue record for this book is available from the British Library.

Design by www.envydesign.co.uk

Printed and bound by CPI Group (UK) Ltd, Croydon, CR0 4YY

1 3 5 7 9 10 8 6 4 2

All images © Wenn except page 249 © Getty Images
and page 250 © PA Photos

Papers used by John Blake Publishing are natural, recyclable
products made from wood grown in sustainable forests.
The manufacturing processes conform to the environmental
regulations of the country of origin.

Every attempt has been made to contact the relevant copyright-
holders, but some were unobtainable. We would be grateful if
the appropriate people could contact us.

For Gee, who shouldn't really
have been watching.

A is for...

Abigail Stock (played by Georgina Moffat)

Abigail appears in the first series and to denote her obvious poshness she ends most of her sentences with the word 'Ya', which causes many of the Roundview pupils she meets to snigger behind her back. As a pupil at the nearby private school, Abigail meets and is instantly attracted to Tony when he visits to sing in the choir. She does her best to steal him from Michelle, and he occasionally sleeps with her. Despite her posh upbringing she swears like a sailor and even Sid, the most articulate of the gang, is shocked by her use of expletives.

After Tony is hit by a car at the end of series one, he

suffers from massive memory loss, so Abigail seizes the opportunity to convince him that she was his girlfriend before the accident. Michelle, his real girlfriend, who is devastated by the accident and can't cope with Tony's inability to remember her, drifts away. Eventually, Sid reveals to Tony that he loved Michelle before the accident, so Abigail is sent packing.

Aimee-Ffion Edwards (plays Sketch)

Much of the *Skins* cast are new to acting, but not so for Aimee-Ffion Edwards. Aimee-Ffion played Sketch in series one and two and has an impressive CV for someone so young. Aimee, who speaks Welsh as well as English, is from Newport in South Wales. She trained as a classical singer and appeared on *Waaffactor*, a 2006 Welsh language TV show. She appeared in the 2002 film *Dwr Dwfn*, and in 2008 made her stage debut at the Trafalgar Studios in London in *SH★T-M★X*. In 2009 she landed a role in *Casualty* for the Valentine's Day episode 'Stand By Me', playing a teenager who becomes involved in a gun-related incident. She also appeared in the original episode of *Casualty 1909* in which she took the part of an abused girl called Deborah Lynch. Aimee-Ffion starred in *Jerusalem* by Jez Butterworth at The Royal Court Theatre in 2009 and reprised her role on Broadway in New York in 2010.

OPPOSITE: AIMEE-FFION EDWARDS.

Alexander Arnold (plays Rich Hardbeck)

In real life Alexander is unrecognisable as his metal-head character, Rich. Part of the third generation of *Skins* characters, Alexander had no previous acting experience and was discovered by the producers in their quest to bring new talent and fresh faces to the series.

In an interview with Cult Box Website, Alex, born in Ashford in Kent, says of his character, 'Rich is very arrogant, he's quite self-absorbed, but at his core he's good-hearted. He just needs some time to decide what he wants. He pours all of his intensity into his music. It's great to play a character that has a lot to talk about.

'A really good friend of mine is into metal music. He was a bit of a reference point. And Jamie Brittain, the show's co-creator, gave me some things I should listen to. The thing is, I can be quite a snob myself with film and music and stuff, so it felt like I just needed to look into myself and see which parts of me were like this character.'

Alexander also had to get used to wearing a wig and heavy biker boots, but he felt they helped him develop a distinctive walk that added credence to the character. He told Cult Box Website: 'The long wig gave me a strange peripheral vision, so I ended up with my head down most of the time and that was a quirk that suited Rich's character.'

At the auditions Alexander hit it off straight away with Will Merrick, who plays Rich's best friend Alo. Both actors feel their friendship was a great help in bonding them to give a convincing portrayal of best mates. 'Our friendship was quite organic. And we just bounce off each other quite well which extends to onscreen as well as off.'

As for the new storylines, Alexander says, 'There are definitely dark waters in this series, but it's probably the lightest series that *Skins* have offered, really. The double-act with Rich and Alo offers a lot of humour, but it's still quite dark in places.'

'Alo' Aloysius Creevey (Played by Will Merrick)

According to the official *Skins* website, ginger-haired, farmer's son Alo lists his favourite things as 'my weed, my van and my dog'. He fits right in at Roundview College where he immediately sets about finding the right girl to help him lose his virginity. He has a penchant for Victorian pornography and no regular girlfriend, claiming to be looking for 'anyone I can get'. He is best friends with Rich, though the two clash constantly over music – Alo likes indie rock bands while Rich loves heavy metal. But the two do agree on one thing: Sex. And lots of it.

Will Merrick – who plays Alo – reveals that it is his first acting job and that he is thrilled to be part of such a popular show. He also loves Alo's sense of humour and his enthusiasm and told the official *Skins* website: 'He's not really trying to be funny. He's got a lot of interaction with a lot of other characters, and he's just a really upbeat kind of guy and so is a very happy part to play.

'He's not living in the city like everyone else; he is living on a big farm just outside Bristol. He's quite a simple minded character who has very basic interests; desperate to start his sexual endeavours, get going with girls and find more friends. He's really interested in getting into the swing of teenage life and embracing it. He's always pushing just to have a great time and is a very positive sort of guy. No task is too hard, and anything is possible with Alo.'

Angie (played by Siwan Morris)

Angie is the youthful and sexy psychology teacher at the college in the first and second series. From the outset there is a forbidden attraction between Angie and her student Chris, who is besotted with her. Initially, Angie fights her desire for one of her pupils as she is shocked by her own feelings. But she eventually gives in and they begin a passionate relationship. In the end, though, Angie goes away and leaves Chris devastated. We learn that she is parted from an estranged fiancé. In series two, Angie revisits Chris and sleeps with him, even though he is now in a relationship with Jal. Realising there is no real future in being with Chris, she goes away once more, leaving her flat to Chris.

Angst (teen)

This German word is a perfect description of the mental state endured from time to time by teenagers, and particularly the characters of *Skins*.

Often thought to mean 'anxiety', angst is rather more complex in meaning. It describes the unbearable anguish of life combined with the desire to overcome the problems of emotional turmoil, raging hormones, fear or rejection and alienation from one's parents. It is defined by crushing loneliness, the uncertainty of friendships, and the need for love.

Anorexia nervosa

Skins has tackled many difficult issues which affect teenagers. Cassie's battle with the life-threatening eating disorder was one of the most poignant and heart-rending storylines of the first and second series. The writers carefully reflected the trauma and worry friends and family go through when close to someone in the grip of the illness and the sufferer's inability to stop harming themselves through starvation. According to the Eating Disorders Association, more than 165,000 people in the UK suffer from anorexia nervosa with 5 per cent of young girls affected.

People with anorexia – which affects women ten times more often than men – starve themselves until they are dangerously ill while still believing they are overweight. They can become very cunning and manipulative, conning those around them into thinking they are eating when they are not. They use all sorts of distraction techniques to fool family and friends and the writers of *Skins* incorporated this into the script.

Cassie seems dreamy and silly when we first meet her, but we soon learn that she is highly controlling when it comes to food and her weight. She has been released from a psychiatric clinic where she has gained weight after becoming dangerously thin, and has been told if she gains a final couple of kilos she can be signed off. Her family and friends believe Cassie is much better, but we see her hiding heavy weights in her underwear just before she goes to be weighed. In another memorable scene, Cassie sits down in front of a large meal at the college cafe and shows Sid how she cons people into thinking she is eating. Cassie cuts up the food and keeps chatting quickly and animatedly. Every time she is about to put her food into her mouth, she quickly asks a question and waves her knife and fork around, distracting Sid. She then cuts up more food and repeats the action fooling Sid into thinking she is eating lots of mouthfuls of food but it is actually the same mouthful over and over again and she never actually eats it. Before he notices the plate is still full, Cassie jumps up saying she is very late for class and scrapes her food onto a plate of a half eaten discarded meal so it is now impossible to see how much Cassie has or hasn't eaten. To complete her deceptive plan, Cassie rubs her tummy and proclaims: 'That was yummy. I'm completely stuffed.' And then rushes off. Sid is impressed yet horrified at her deception and skill.

KAYA AND HANNAH MURRAY (RIGHT) WHO PLAYS ANOREXIC CASSIE IN
SERIES ONE AND TWO.

Anwar Kharral (played by Dev Patel)

One of the most loveable and complicated characters from the first and second series is Anwar, a fresh-faced Muslim with large sticking-out ears who cannot quite reconcile his desire for sex and drugs with his faith. Describing himself as 'young, brown (and I know how to get down)', he is often labelled as a 'pick and choose' Muslim. He prays five times a day and regularly attends Mosque with his family, yet claims that his favourite things are tequila, breasts, dope, pills and *The X Factor*. He is also desperate to lose his virginity.

Anwar's best friend is Maxxie, but he has difficulty coming to terms with him being gay. On the day of Anwar's 17th birthday party, Maxxie rings him to wish him happy birthday, but says that he will not attend the festivities unless Anwar's parents know that he is gay. Anwar is not enjoying the party without Maxxie and to make matters worse one of his ageing uncles is acting as DJ and no one is dancing or enjoying the old-fashioned music. Anwar and Maxxie meet outside the party hall where Mr Kharral, Anwar's father, spots them talking. As Mr Kharral chats to Maxxie, Anwar blurts out that Maxxie is gay. Mr Kharral seems oblivious, so Maxxie repeats the statement. In a very moving moment, Mr Kharral, explains that homosexuals are something he does not understand, but would never discriminate against, as he has faith that God will one day enlighten him about why gay people are the way they are. Much to Maxxie and Anwar's astonishment, it is obvious that Mr Kharral has known all along.

According to fellow actor Mike Bailey, who plays Sid, the characterisation of Anwar was partly based on the personality of Dev Patel, the actor who plays him. The role was written for Dev after he was selected to join the cast.

Sexually, things look up for Anwar when he starts dating Sketch, only to discover she is in fact obsessed with Maxxie – she even looks at a picture of him whilst having sex with Anwar. Sketch persuades Anwar to bleach his hair blonde and wear clothes like Maxxie but, eventually, Anwar realises that she is trying to mould him into a Maxxie clone and gives her the elbow.

The gang pledge to open their A level results together, but Anwar cannot resist having a sneaky peek and is horrified to see he has failed his exams. Unable to go to his friends or his family, Anwar visits Sketch who tells him that he never gave any thought to his future. She also tries to manipulate Anwar into getting back together with her by suggesting that his friends will move on and leave him behind.

Frightened for his future, Anwar goes to bid Maxxie farewell at Bristol coach station. Maxxie is heading for a life in London with his new boyfriend James. Suddenly, Maxxie suggests Anwar comes with them and have a ball in London. Without a moment's thought (or a suitcase) Anwar jumps on the bus with a giant grin on his face.

THE GORGEOUS
DEV PATEL PLAYS
THE LOVEABLE
CHARACTER ANWAR.

April Pearson (plays Michelle Richardson)

Since the tender age of three, April Pearson has acted with a Bristol theatre group. Throughout her childhood and youth she starred in many school plays and drama group productions.

April made her television debut in 1998 with a part in *Casualty* before going on to star in *Skins*. Encouraged by her drama teacher, she got the part when casting directors held auditions at her school. Although the main characters of *Skins* are replaced every two series, creators Jamie Brittain and Bryan Elsley were so impressed with April's work that they have considered bringing Michelle back (along with other original old characters) for occasional appearances. In 2008 Pearson appeared for the second time in *Casualty* as a character called Karen. She made her film debut in the 2009 movie *Tormented*, playing the part of Tasha, a sadistic schoolgirl along with *Skins* co-star Larissa Wilson, who took the role of Khalillah, the most popular girl at school. Total Film reviewed it as, 'a slasher for the *Skins* generation'.

Early in 2009, Pearson returned to theatre to star in the Bristol Old Vic production *Suspension* and in the autumn of the same year played a teenager called Callie in *Negative Space* at New End Theatre.

Arabella Weir (plays Anna Richardson)

The British comedienne, actress and writer made a memorable cameo appearance in series one and two as

Michelle's mother Anna. Much to Michelle's annoyance, hopeless romantic Anna is always searching for Mr Right but has a tendency to pick the wrong men. This lands Michelle with a succession of unsuitable step-fathers (or, as she calls them 'toyboy/business failure/serial idiots'). Weir is best known for her roles in *The Fast Show* and for writing several books including the international bestseller *Does My Bum Look Big in This* (her catchphrase from many hilarious sketches in *The Fast Show*). She guest-starred in two series of *Skins* and, although her character exasperated her daughter Michelle, they had a loving relationship — unlike most of the teens and parents in the show.

Ardal O'Hanlon (plays Kieran)

Probably best known as the loveable and naive priest Father Dougall in sitcom *Father Ted*, this gifted actor guest stars as Kieran, the hapless politics lecturer at Roundview in series three. Having long since lost all passion for his job, Kieran is often heard declaring that he hates teaching. Indeed, he does little to inspire the students. The college has made a number of futile attempts to reignite his love for teaching by sending him on motivational courses, but Kieran's main motivation seems to be trying to get Naomi into bed.

Ardal was born in Carrickmacross, Ireland, and is the son of Rory O'Hanlon, an Irish politician and doctor. His grandfather, Michael O'Hanlon, was a member of the IRA and part of Michael Collins' squad which assassinated

APRIL
PEARSON.

THE VERY FUNNY ARDAL O'HANLON.

British secret service agents in Dublin on Bloody Sunday in 1920.

After graduating with a degree in Communications Studies, O'Hanlon founded the International Comedy Cellar in Dublin along with Kevin Gildea and Barry Murphy. Ardal found fame as a stand-up comedian after winning the Hackney Empire New Act of the Year competition in 1994. Later, he presented *The Stand Up Show* and was in the award-winning short film *Flying Saucer Rock'n'Roll*. He began straight acting roles with Emma Fielding and Beth Goddard in the ITV comedy-drama *Big Bad World*.

In 2000, O'Hanlon starred in *My Hero*, a comedy series in which he played a superhero from the planet Ultron. In 2005, he played character Coconut Tam in the film *The Adventures of Greyfriars Bobby*.

Autism

Through the character of JJ in series three, *Skins* introduces the audience to the condition of autism and how it affects those who suffer from it. Autism is a lifelong developmental disorder – those who have it often have great difficulty understanding and relating to others. Taking part in everyday social and family life can be very challenging. The disorder can vary from very mild to so severe that the people affected are completely unable to take part in normal society. Autism is believed to affect more than 580,000 people in the UK.

JJ has high-functioning autism. On the surface he seems no different — he has friends and is studying at a mainstream college. However, he has trouble understanding the actions and motives of his contemporaries and finds social interaction harder than most. He often blurts out the truth at inappropriate times and is prone to rages that lead him to break material things like the toys and superhero figures that are precious to him. JJ needs medication to help him stay calm.

JJ is gentle, thoughtful and highly intelligent, but at times very unhappy about his condition. He is teased by kids on the street and keeps asking himself why he is not 'normal'. He finds an answer of sorts in one poignant episode when he realises all his friends are messed up and hating each other because none of them is prepared to tell the truth. 'Actually, I am the normal one,' he whispers to himself.

Awards

For the actors and production team who work on *Skins* there is no better recognition than being nominated for an award, let alone winning one. And, despite having come under fire for controversial scenes, *Skins* has had the last laugh when it comes to award ceremonies.

The series scooped the coveted Best Drama prize at the 2008 Rose d'Or global television festival and the Best Production Design Award at the 2008 Royal Television Society Awards, where it was also nominated for Best Drama Photography.

When watching the opening credits, be aware that that Britain's most prestigious film and TV establishment honoured the show with Best Title Sequence at the British Academy Television Craft Awards in 2008. It was also nominated for Best Drama Series in 2008 but lost out to *The Street*. Devoted fans then put their money where their mouths were and picked up the phone to vote helping *Skins* scoop the coveted Philips Audience Award at the BAFTAs in 2009.

More accolades were heaped on the show in 2010 when it was nominated as Outstanding Drama Series during the 21st GLAAD Media Awards.

B is for...

Bristol

Skins is filmed almost entirely in Bristol and centres on the pupils of Roundview sixth-form college. The production team have used the real-life schools and colleges Henbury School, John Cabot Academy and Filton College as backgrounds for Roundview and locations in and around the city are instantly recognisable to Bristolians. Bristol is a sprawling, bustling, happening city with a large population of students, and its bars and nightclubs make the perfect backdrop for the hedonistic cast of the teen drama. Many scenes are also shot in the beautiful surrounding countryside. Several waterways run through the city, and the potential for swimming has given the cast yet more excuses to strip off.

Co-creator Jamie Brittain admits that *Skins* is filmed on a tight budget, which means there isn't much money around for classy, high definition shots of the city. Jamie told TelevisionaryWebsite, 'The city is very important to the show and we chose a city like Bristol because it's big enough to have a lot of interesting places to go to but small enough to have sort of a community centre to it. The word Bristol is rarely used in the show and we've only ever used the Clifton Suspension Bridge once, which is a big landmark. I like to think that the city is sort of a strange, unknowable place in *Skins* and the characters move through it in a slightly confused sense. Certainly, if you watch some of the episodes in series three, the city is much more of a character and there's many more weird places to go to.'

Some real-life Bristol pupils have complained that the depiction of the show's students in their city is unrealistic, too sensationalist and does not reflect their own experiences. While admitting to being fans of the show and enjoying its shenanigans, some have expressed concerns over scenes depicting sex and drugs within the walls of Roundview College. At a preview of the third series of the show, one group of students laughed out loud at many scenes – they enjoyed the show but claimed that – unlike the characters – none of them ever drank lager or smoked spliffs at eight o'clock in the morning.

C is for...

C word

Until quite recently, the C word was never heard on television, but, these days, it is slowly closing in on 'fuck' in the obscenity stakes and is frequently used in *Skins*. Despite the critics who have deplored its use, the history of the word is interesting. It was in common usage from the Middle Ages until the eighteenth century. After a period of disuse in Victorian times, usage became more frequent in the twentieth century.

Cannabis

Barely a scene goes by without a spliff making an appearance. The characters seem to have an endless supply of the stuff and smoke it with abandon morning, noon and night. Even the name *Skins* refers to the slang name of the cigarette papers used to roll a joint.

Critics have claimed that the show condones illegal drug taking and ignores the dangers of cannabis smoking. In defence of the show actor Nicholas Hoult (who plays Tony) feels that, though based in truth, many scenes in the show have been sensationalised for dramatic and comedic reasons – he urges viewers not to take every scene too literally.

Cassie Ainsworth (played by Hannah Murray)

When she makes her appearance as Michelle's mixed-up, anorexic friend in the very first episode we discover that 18-year-old Cassie has just been released from a psychiatric hospital. She suffers from a host of mental disorders that include anorexia nervosa, low self-esteem, suicidal ideation and drug addiction. Cassie is as thin as a blade of grass, and has an irritating habit of saying 'wow' a lot. She's a permanent car accident that should cause people to avoid her like a dose of bubonic plague. And yet there is a vulnerable, loveable quality about her that makes you care even as her self-destructive behaviour is breaking your heart. No wonder Sid comes to love her. If she had a personal theme song it would have to be '*Candle in the Wind*'. One reviewer described Cassie as being 'as pale as Hamlet's Ophelia and arguably twice as mad'.

BEAUTIFUL HANNAH LOOKING EVERY INCH LIKE HER QUIRKY *SKINS* CHARACTER CASSIE.

Hannah Murray, who plays Cassie, describes her character as 'very interesting because she has a lot of problems, and she's very troubled, and she's anorexic and completely lacking in self-esteem and self-belief, but along with that she's sort of quite smart.'

We first meet Cassie when she has just been discharged from hospital after a suicide attempt. Her best friend Michelle arranges for her to take Sid's virginity at a party. It doesn't happen, but throughout the first series, Cassie develops an attraction to Sid, who unintentionally stands her up twice. After he does this for the first time, she attempts suicide again and, when he does it again (in order to rescue his best friend Tony's sister Effy from overdosing), Cassie decides to move to Scotland to take further treatment. She postpones her plans after discovering Sid loves her. The first series ends with reconciliation with Sid on the night she is heading north.

The second episode of the first series and the penultimate episode of the second series focus on Cassie. The first of these concentrates on her mental state and the next examines her relationship with roommate Chris Miles (played by Joe Dempsie).

In an interview with *The Independent*, the show's writers described the first episode devoted to Cassie as being about 'how she gets through her day without eating ... how she feels and what her tactics are'. In one clever scene, she demonstrates how to give the impression of eating a plate of food by cutting up what's on her plate and at the same time carrying out an animated conversation that distracts from the fact that she isn't eating anything at all.

In the second series, Cassie, in Scotland, communicates with Sid by webcam. The relationship is shattered when Sid sees Cassie on a bed with a gay male friend and imagines she has been unfaithful. The relationship is strained further when Mark (Sid's father) dies. Sid heads for Scotland to find Cassie, but she is already travelling back to Bristol to meet him. Their trains pass. Distraught by Cassie's disappearance and in emotional turmoil caused by his father's death, Sid begins a relationship with Michelle.

Because of Sid's new relationship with Michelle, Cassie becomes more mentally unstable while taking shelter in Chris's flat. Cassie's promiscuous behaviour with men and women leads to Chris losing his job with an estate agent, which in turn causes trouble between him and his girlfriend Jal.

Cassie blames her addiction to 'mindless sex' on her failed relationship with Sid. When Sid realises what has happened to her, he confronts Cassie about her promiscuity. He says he is sorry for dating Michelle, and tells Cassie he really loves her.

Cassie tells Sid she will love him forever but after witnessing her friend Chris suffering from two subarachnoid haemorrhages, the second of which kills him, she is so shattered she runs away to New York. In the Big Apple she meets a decent young man called Adam and they form a powerful platonic friendship. He offers to put her up in his apartment. Subsequently Adam leaves the apartment to find his ex-girlfriend and Cassie gets a job as a waitress at Adam's favourite diner.

In the last episode of series two, Sid and Cassie make their final appearances, which is in keeping with *Skins* tradition that characters only run for two seasons. Sid decides not to give up on Cassie and heads to New York to track her down. We witness Sid wandering through the streets of Manhattan showing her photograph to asking passers-by. The episode ends with him turning back to look inside the diner where Cassie works and we feel sure they will meet again.

Chris Addison (plays Headmaster David Blood)

This highly respected stand-up comic and star of *The Thick of It* took a cameo role as Headmaster David Blood in series four. Describing his character as a control freak and an uptight, smug bully, Chris, 38, also admitted to feeling ancient among the young cast.

'I think *Skins* makes anyone above the age of 23 feel old,' he said. 'That's one of its great strengths. It's energetic, colourful and full of life in a way that not much drama is on TV these days. It's a combination of fun and terrifying to watch if you're out of its immediate demographic – particularly terrifying if you're a parent of teenagers.'

CONTROL FREAK HEADMASTER DAVID BLOOD PLAYED BY THE VERY FUNNY CHRIS ADDISON.

Chris Miles (played by Joe Dempsie)

At the start of series one, Chris is portrayed as only being interested in drugs, sex and having a good time, but there is more to his personality and interesting reasons for his behaviour. The official *Skins* website says Chris will 'smoke and snort anything, screw or rob anyone'. The only thing he is serious about is his psychology lessons, but only because he is infatuated with Angie, his teacher, who Chris thinks is 'out of this world'. To his frustration, he even sees Angie naked in the teachers' showers (where he is using their superior hair dryer).

Chris idolised his brother, who died from a subarachnoid haemorrhage, and feels he will never be as good as he was, or live up to his memory in his mother's eyes. He lives alone with his mother as his father left long ago.

One morning Chris discovers his mother has run away and left him £1,000. Chris wastes no time in frittering it away on drugs and also buys some music equipment, which he soon wrecks.

With the last of his money, Chris buys some Viagra and throws a wild party and invites Angie. She turns up but is uncomfortable to discover she is the only teacher present. Angie dances reluctantly with Chris, but his Viagra experiment has left him with an ever-present erection – Angie soon brushes against it and, outraged, flees the party.

Chris's life continues to spiral out of control. He sells all his furniture to raise money and is living in squalor. He wakes up naked one morning to find a squatter in his bath. The squatter claims he now possesses the property and –

JOE DEMPSIE PLAYED THE POPULAR CHARACTER CHRIS MILES.

still naked – Chris is kicked out of his own house. He walks to school naked and goes to Angie for help and advice where his friends arrive and give him clothes.

Jal takes Chris to see his estranged dad who makes it clear he doesn't want anything to do with his son. During the visit, Chris accidentally drops his baby half-brother before fleeing the house with Jal. Chris makes for the graveyard and, once there, he sits on a gravestone and tells Jal about the best day of his life – he describes how he was in the Scouts and his older brother Peter paid him loads of attention and he didn't have a care in the world. Chris finishes the story and stands up to reveal that he has been sitting on his older brother's gravestone.

Things begin to look up for Chris when Angie gives him a college dorm room. What's more, when they go on a college trip to Russia together, Chris sticks up for Angie during a row with another teacher and Angie thanks him with a kiss and this leads to sex.

In the first episode of the second series, Chris, Maxxie and Jal comfort Tony, who has changed completely since he was run over. That night, they go to a party without telling Tony because they know he is unable to take drugs due to his brain injury.

In the next episode, we learn that Angie has decided not to return to Roundview College. Angie leaves a message to her students, and part of it is a coded sentence to Chris which indicates the possibility of a reunion. Nonetheless, Chris is still upset.

Jal persuades Chris to sort his life out and he gets a job

as an estate agent, which enables him to squat in a flat he is unable to sell.

Cassie moves in and Chris and Jal get together, and Chris's life begins to take on a normal pattern. Chris excels in the job, and he and Jal are a happy couple. But Jal is keeping a secret – she is pregnant with his baby.

In a tragic twist, Chris suffers a subarachnoid haemorrhage – the result of a hereditary condition that killed his brother. Jal tells an unconscious Chris she is pregnant and presents him with her lucky coin to protect him during his operation.

Initially, Chris seems to make a good recovery but in the last episode he suffers a second stroke and dies. His father blames Chris's friends for his son's degenerate lifestyle and forbids them from attending the funeral. Consequently, Tony and Sid steal the body from the undertaker's hearse to hold their own funeral service for Chris. This infuriates Jal and Michelle, who persuade the boys to return the coffin. In the end, Chris's friends watch the funeral from afar, and Jal makes a speech comparing Chris to Captain Joe Kittinger, one of his heroes. The assembled friends set off a battery of fireworks that fill the twilight sky. They have said their own farewell.

Clare Grogan (plays Mini's mum)

Glasgow-born Clare Grogan is an actress and singer who was discovered by director Bill Forsyth and played a schoolgirl in his film *Gregory's Girl*. Grogan played Charlotte in Forsyth's

CLARE GROGAN WAS AN EXCELLENT CAST ADDITION AS MINI'S MUM.

Comfort and Joy and had parts in *Blott on the Landscape* and *Red Dwarf*. She has also appeared in *Father Ted* and *Eastenders*. She is the lead singer of Altered Images and the band has had a series of hits. Grogan is married to fellow band member Stephen Lironi, they live in the London borough of Haringey with their adopted daughter. Grogan has published a children's novel titled *Tallulah and the Teenstars*, is a devoted supporter of Celtic FC and sports a scar on the left side of her face after an accident involving a broken glass when she was 17. Clare is a patron of the British Association for Adoption and Fostering.

In the fifth series of *Skins*, Clare takes the role of Mini's mum Shelley, a single parent obsessed with keeping her body beautiful. She has ambitions for Mini, and wants her to achieve something in life rather than simply being used by men.

Cook. James Cook (played by Jack O'Connell)

It's hard not to have an opinion about Cook, the larger-than-life antihero of series three and four. Love him or hate him, he's guaranteed to keep you watching.

From the outset, Cook bursts onto the screen swigging lager and getting stoned as he arrives for his first day at college. Before the day is over, Effy had challenged Cook to break all the rules the head teacher has set, and Cook has duly dropped his trousers in front of the whole year, sworn at teachers, taken drugs and had sex on the college premises.

We learn very quickly that Cook is an outlandish extrovert and highly promiscuous with a very big self-destruct button. Although he has been best friends with Freddie and JJ since childhood – they call themselves The Three Musketeers – in the first episode of series three we learn that Cook has been trying the patience of his two closest friends and their relationship has become strained. This is further tested by Cook setting out to seduce Effy, whom Freddie has fallen for. All three boys are attracted to Effy and throughout series three and four, her manipulation and sexual teasing of all three continues to drive a wedge between them.

Although Cook claims to never care about anything and can often be heard shouting his catchphrase – 'I'm Cook, I'm Cook, I don't give a fuck' – the viewer learns that, underneath the arrogance and bravado, Cook has a soft heart that has been broken by his troubled background and selfish parents. It is this pain that causes him to act out. Although he falls in love with Effy, his true loves are Freddie and JJ. Although he seems unable to stop causing them heartache, he is desperately sad that their friendship is no longer what it was.

Cook also has a bigger appetite for drugs and sex than most of the other characters put together. His pursuit of hedonistic drug-fuelled nights and endless sexual partners covers up his need for acceptance and integrity.

Throughout series three, we follow Cook on a spiral of self-destruction as he alienates pretty much everyone around him. He takes on the local gangster (after stealing from him when he is tied up in a seedy brothel), has constant fights, habitually cheats on Effy and seduces the vulnerable Pandora, which almost destroys her relationship with Thomas. By the last episode of series three it seems that Cook has no friends left and – after going on the run with Effy after she attacks Katie while high on magic mushrooms – Cook heads in search of his father, his 'hero'. But it turns out that his dad is a washed up loser living on a filthy boat and drinking himself stupid. Effy contacts JJ and Freddie to come and help get Cook away from his father. After witnessing Cook being violently threatened by him they all realise why Cook is such a mess.

Cook's life takes an even darker turn in series four when he ends up in prison after being charged with GBH. He is also suffering guilt for dealing drugs to Sophia, a young girl who commits suicide whilst high on MDMA. Cook is released on an electronic tag and briefly moves in with his vain and drunken mother, a famous artist. He begins to bond with his younger brother Paddy, who idolises him. When Cook sees Paddy emulating his aggressive and arrogant behaviour, he realises he has to change his life, goes to his lawyer and confesses to dealing the drugs to Sophia. He is imprisoned yet again.

Life takes a further tragic turn when Freddie goes missing. Unbeknownst to the gang, Freddie has been murdered by Effy's psychopathic doctor John Foster. Desperately worried about Freddie's whereabouts, Cook – who has escaped from prison – has an instinct Foster

JAMES 'I'M COOK'
COOK PLAYED BY
CHEEKY CHAP JACK
O'CONNELL.

has hurt Freddie. He breaks into Foster's house and finds bloodstained clothes and shoes. Foster attacks him with a baseball bat and in his final act of bravery Cook tells Foster he knows he killed Freddie. It is obvious that Cook intends to kill Foster in revenge for Freddie's death. His last words as he launches himself at him are the haunting and very apt: 'I'm Cook.' As this is where series four ends, and is the last we see of the characters of series three and four, we are left to make up our own minds about what happens to Cook.

Critics

'Disgusting', 'degenerate', 'horrifying' and 'irresponsible' were just some of the words used by critics when *Skins* was first aired on E4 in 2007.

Although the British public have come a long way since the 1970s, when Mary Whitehouse wanted to ban Dr Who, the antics of Tony and his gang definitely got everyone talking.

Huge media coverage before the show had even aired meant the first episode was watched by 1.6 million viewers – a then record for E4.

Creator of the show Bryan Elsley expected criticism yet stands by his work declaring on MTV News:

Skins is a very simple and in fact rather old-fashioned television series. It's about the lives and loves of teenagers, how they get through high school, how they deal with their friends, and also how they circumnavigate some of the complications of sex, relationships, educations, parents, drugs and alcohol.

In the UK, viewers and commentators very quickly realised that, although there are some sensational aspects to the show, *Skins* is actually a very serious attempt to get to the roots of young people's lives. It deals with relationships, parents, death, illness, mental health issues, the consequences of drug use and sexual activity. It is just that these are characterised from the point of view of the many young people who write the show and has a very straightforward approach to their experiences; it tries to tell the truth. Sometimes that truth can be a little painful to adults and parents.

D is for...

Dakota Blue Richards (plays Franky Fitzgerald)

Dakota Blue Richards is the most experienced actress in the fifth series of *Skins* – she played Lyra alongside Nicole Kidman and Daniel Craig in *The Golden Compass*. Philip Pullman (author of the book *The Golden Compass* is based on) said 'I knew the search was over for Lyra' when he saw Dakota's screen test.

Born in South Kensington, London, Richards grew up in Brighton and has made two other movies – *Dustbin Baby* and *The Secret of Moonacre*. She went to K-BIS Theatre School, one of Sussex's premier drama schools, and now (like her on-screen character) attends sixth-form college.

Richards is due to appear in a thriller, *Lovely to the Last*, and in a film called *Rain*. She said in an interview with *The*

DAKOTA FOUND FAME AS A YOUNG GIRL AND STARRED ALONGSIDE
NICOLE KIDMAN IN *THE GOLDEN COMPASS*.

Times how proud she was of herself for working very hard to keep active within show business. In series five of *Skins*, Richards plays Franky Fitzgerald, a clever but reticent teenage girl. Because of her unusually androgynous dress sense (she wears men's suits and greases back her hair), Franky initially finds it hard to fit in among her more fashion-conscious peers. She arrives late at Roundview College, and has been bullied at her previous school. Of her part, Richards told We Love Brighton.Com:

'It's crazy to be part of this *Skins* phenomenon; it's as much a lifestyle choice as anything because of the attention that comes with it.

'In terms of my role I've had a different upbringing, more stable and secure than Franky's. We don't know much about her past but we assume it's a dark one which adds to her enigmatic character.

'She has two adoptive dads, and her past shows through as she develops through the series. She would be the most interesting friend to have out of all the *Skins* characters; I'd definitely get on with her. She tries to be outside clichés and doesn't want to be popular or noticed.

'I've always been a big fan of *Skins* and it's important that people can relate to the experiences shown in the programme so they can say, "Yes that happened to me." In the drama things will be more hardcore than reality but they are also relatable and fun.'

Danny Dyer (plays Malcolm, Michelle's stepfather)

Playing against his usual hard-man type, Danny Dyer makes some memorable appearances in series one as Malcolm, Michelle's stepfather. Michelle cannot understand why her mother Anna has married yet another loser, but we soon learn that Malcolm is reputed to be very well endowed. The marriage quickly hits the buffers after Malcolm buys some hideous toys and decorates the house with them. Snobbish interior designer Anna is horrified by his bad taste and realises he is not the man for her.

Dyer broke into the mainstream after starring in the 1999 movie *Human Traffic*, a cult film which explored drug culture, the dramas of coming of age and nightclubbing. This and his subsequent performances in *Borstal Boy*, *The Football Factory* and *The Business* established Dyer as an actor popular amongst adults and teenagers alike. His 2008 TV documentary series *Danny Dyer's Deadliest Men* saw him entering the dark depths of the British underworld and interviewing some of the country's hardened criminals.

Born in 1977 in London's tough East End, and a dedicated West Ham United fan, Dyer now lives in Essex with his long-time girlfriend Joanne Mas and two young daughters. Starring in *Skins* opened Dyer's eyes to the sex and drugs culture of teenagers today.

In an interview with the *Sun* newspaper, he said with a chuckle: 'Having daughters has frightened the life out of me. My 40s are going to be a very stressful time. I will

DANNY DYER.

probably spend them running around with a baseball bat looking for the blokes who have upset my girls.'

David Baddiel (plays Jim Stonem's boss)

David appears in series three of *Skins* as the boss of Jim Stonem, Tony and Effy's dad. He soon begins a passionate affair with their mum Anthea (played by Baddiel's real-life partner Morwenna Banks).

Born in New York, Baddiel moved to England when he was four months old. His mother, Sarah, was a refugee from Nazi Germany. Baddiel grew up in Dollis Hill, North London and read English at King's College, Cambridge, where he was a member of the Cambridge Footlights, and graduated with a double first.

He began studies for a PhD in English at University College London, but decided instead to become a stand-up comedian and a writer for various radio programmes. His first television appearance came in an episode of showbiz satire *Filthy, Rich and Catflap*. In 1988, he met Rob Newman, a comic impressionist, and the two formed a writing partnership. They wrote a comedy show for BBC Radio 1 called *The Mary Whitehouse Experience* which led to highly successful television work.

Baddiel co-hosted Channel 4's *A Stab In The Dark* with Michael Gove and Tracey MacLeod. Baddiel teamed up with Newman again for the *Newman and Baddiel in Pieces* series in 1993. Eventually, the pair broke up with some acrimony after a sell-out appearance at Wembley Arena.

COMEDIAN DAVID BADDIEL.

After taking in comedian Frank Skinner as a lodger at his London apartment, the pair subsequently worked together on the show *Fantasy Football League*. Next they took an improvised show to the Edinburgh Festival which became the TV series, *Baddiel and Skinner Unplanned*.

Baddiel has written three novels: *Time For Bed*, *Whatever Love Means* and *The Secret Purposes*. He is patron of the Campaign Against Living Miserably (CALM).

Dev Patel (plays Anwar Kharral)

There is no greater *Skins* success story than Dev's. Just two years after winning the role of Anwar, Dev was attending the Oscars as the star of worldwide smash hit *Slumdog Millionaire*. Just 18, Dev was walking the red carpet with a stunning girlfriend on his arm and bearing a smile as wide as the ocean. But none of it would have happened if he hadn't have played Anwar.

Struggling to cast his leading man, *Slumdog Millionaire* director Danny Boyle turned to his teenage daughter for help. He had originally begun his search in Bollywood but felt that the buff, strong and traditionally handsome actors were wrong for the part of Jamal Malik. His daughter Caitlin pointed him towards Dev – five nerve-wracking auditions later, he had won the role.

Even then he had no idea the movie would take the world by storm and dominate the 2009 Academy Awards with Dev up for Best Actor for his very first film role. *Slumdog Millionaire* was nominated for ten Oscars and scooped eight. Although he lost out to Sean Penn, Dev would receive a number of awards for his performance, including a British Independent Film Award, National Board of Review (NBR) Award, Chicago Film Critics Association Award and two Black Reel Awards for Best Actor and Best Breakthrough Performance

It was an astonishing achievement for an actor of barely any experience and Dev admitted that on the first day of filming *Skins* he didn't really know what to do. He grew up in Harrow, north west London, and had never acted before *Skins* – he was only persuaded to go to the audition by his mum (even though he had a science exam the next day!). Dev managed to pass four A Levels while playing Anwar and is now a hugely sought after star.

Rather ironically for the boy who had played unlucky in love Anwar in *Skins*, Dev won the heart of his beautiful co-star Freida Pinto whilst filming *Slumdog Millionaire*. The two remain together today.

Dev will always be hugely grateful for the chance to play Anwar, but he does admit to sometimes feeling slightly embarrassed by the hormonal teenager's antics. 'It's not the sort of thing you should sit down and watch with your parents and I made the mistake of doing that,' he admits with a loud chuckle in an interview with the Daily Mirror.

'I was literally buck-naked throughout the whole of the second series which was mortifying – so embarrassing. To my mum and dad I'm still a baby and they were surprised that their little son was doing all these crazy scenes. They

DEV BECAME AN INTERNATIONAL SUPER STAR AFTER TAKING ON THE LEAD ROLE IN SLUMDOG MILLIONAIRE AND HE ALSO GOT HIMSELF A BEAUTIFUL GIRLFRIEND, ACTRESS FREIDA PINTO.

weren't at all angry – they know it's just acting – although mum did say, 'Don't bring that character home.'

Dev is good friends with Nicholas Hoult, another star of *Skins* to have achieved Hollywood acclaim. He admits that they hooked up in LA but – being under 21 – were too young to go out drinking. Instead, they stayed in the hotel and raided the mini bar.

Doug (played by Giles Thomas)

Doug is a biology teacher at the college and the headteacher's chief henchman. He's a confused figure whose customary need to be liked by the pupils is occasionally interrupted by flashes of authoritarianism. On the whole, he is treated with amiable contempt by the student body, but never with the outright hostility they usually reserve for adults. His most memorable moment was when he held the megaphone behind his back and produced a series of spectacular farts (which he explains have been caused by a surfeit of rhubarb in his diet).

When Bruce Gelcar, the drama teacher (played by Shane Richie) is fired after Sketch falsely accuses him of sexual harassment, Doug takes over the school's production of *Osama! The Musical*. He also steps in to take over Angie's psychology class when she flees from the emotional entrapment of her affair with Chris.

Douglas Hodge (plays Edward Jones, JJ's father)

Douglas Hodge makes a cameo appearance as JJ's father Edward in the fourth series. Hodge trained for the stage at the Royal Academy of Dramatic Art. He is a council member of the National Youth Theatre; Hodge has achieved great success on stage in plays by Harold Pinter. He has two children with his partner, actress Tessa Peake-Jones. Hodge has a fine singing voice and has appeared in musicals as well as many television productions.

Dudley Sutton (plays Norman, Freddie's grandfather)

As Effy becomes increasingly depressed, Freddie goes to visit his grandfather Norman in his nursing home and expresses his concern over Effy's psychotic behaviour. Norman reveals that his own daughter – Freddie's mum – suffered from the same illness, which eventually led to her suicide. He warns Freddie that he must seek professional help for Effy.

Dudley Sutton was born in Surrey and learned his craft at the Royal Academy of Dramatic Art. He married actress Marjorie Steele before becoming a cult figure because of his role as a gay biker in 1964 movie *The Leather Boys.* Sutton and Steele had a child but divorced in 1965. He played the title role in the first production of Joe Orton's groundbreaking play, *Entertaining Mr Sloane* in 1963. His many film roles include *Crossplot, Rotten to the*

DOUGLAS HODGE.

KATE MOLLOY

Core, Madame Sin, The Devils, The Pink Panther Strikes Again, Edward II and *The Football Factory*. Among his many television appearances were roles in *Lovejoy, The Beiderbecke Trilogy*, and *Smiley's People*. He received acclaim for his performance as *William Blake*, in Peter Ackroyd's BBC production. He lives in Chelsea, London.

DUDLEY SUTTON.

E is for...

Ecstasy

Every time *Skins* sets the action of the show in a club, a party, or a rave, we see the enthusiastic and liberal consumption of Ecstasy, either in pill or powder form. Effy even bakes it into a cake at Pandora's pyjama party. This led to criticisms of the first and second series, and the show was accused of glamorising the drug. But in the second series, Naomi and Cook give Ecstasy to a girl called Sophia and as a result she commits suicide.

According to the website FRANK (www.talktofrank.com), a national drug education service set up by the Department of Health, Ecstasy– also often called MDMA in the show – is the original designer drug. Clubbers take it because it gives them an energy buzz and enables them to stay awake and continue to dance, literally, for hours. Ecstasy makes people feel pleased with their surroundings and it intensifies sounds and colours. The effects kick in after about half an hour of taking the drug and last for up to six hours, leading to a gradual comedown. Slang names for drugs can vary around the country: Mitsubishis, E, pills, Dolphins, Brownies, Rolex's, Mandy, and XTC.

Ecstasy has often been welcomed because it does not produce the violence often associated with alcohol; in fact it often makes the user feel love for those around them, be it friends or strangers. The dangers in taking the drug are worrying. You can build up a tolerance, so that you need more to gain the same effect and psychological dependency can develop. There are uncertainties about the long-term side effects. FRANK says that it may cause brain damage and problems such as personality change, memory loss, and depression. Ecstasy is a Class A drug. It is illegal to possess it, give it away or sell it. Possession makes you liable to seven years in jail. Supplying someone else, even including your friends, can technically lead to a life sentence and an unlimited fine. Known to chemists as MDMA, pure Ecstasy is a white crystalline powder. Commonly sold on the street as tablets, it is increasingly being sold as a powder. On the website, some of the short-term side effects of taking Ecstasy are listed as: anxiety, panic attacks, and confused, paranoid or psychotic states. Ecstasy also affects the body's temperature control. Dancing for long periods in a hot atmosphere increases the chances of overheating and dehydration. Users should take regular breaks from the dance floor to cool down. Ecstasy can cause the body to release a hormone that prevents the production of urine. Drink too quickly and it interferes with your body's salt balance, which can be as deadly as not drinking enough water. According to FRANK, using Ecstasy has been linked to liver, kidney and heart problems. Some long-term users report getting colds, flu and sore throats more often. This may be attributed to staying awake for 24 hours, which puts the immune system under pressure. There've been over 200 ecstasy–related deaths in the UK since 1996.

Effy 'Elizabeth' Stonem (played by Kaya Scodelario)

Beautiful, enigmatic, manipulative and at times a complete bitch, Effy Stonem is one of the most watchable and compelling characters created for *Skins*. As the sister of Tony (the hero of series one and two) Effy makes brief but significant appearances in the first two series. Tony seems proud of his wayward little sister who, despite being only 14, regularly stays out all night clubbing. He constantly distracts his parents so they don't catch her out.

The very last scene of series two shows Effy lying under Tony's legendary 'naked bodies' duvet cover. As the camera pans in for a close-up, Effy smiles suggestively into the camera as if to say 'Now it's my turn to cause merry hell at Roundview College.'

Effy inherits Tony's role as the most popular kid at

college from the moment she arrives at Roundview. Almost instantly, Freddie, Cook and JJ fall for her feminine wiles. Effy drives a wedge through their once unbreakable friendship (sometimes intentionally, sometimes not) throughout series three and four.

On day one of college, the head teacher warns pupils that they will be instantly expelled if they are caught taking drugs, having sex, looking at pornography, sniffing glue or committing arson. Effy bats her eyelids flirtatiously at Freddie, who is smitten. Just when he thinks she might agree to go out with him, Effy, realising all three boys want her, exclaims that the one who breaks all the rules first can have her. Cook accepts the challenge wholeheartedly and before the day is out he is smoking a spliff and having wild sex with Effy in the college medical room. Freddie is hurt but keeps his feelings to himself. At first Cook is oblivious and pursues an on-off sexual relationship with Effy. It soon becomes clear that both boys have fallen deeply in love with her. For the remainder of series three (although she actually loves Freddie), Effy continues to play the two friends off against each other.

Effy begins series three as a sexually experienced girl. She appears cool, mysterious and constantly in control, but underneath her apparent devil-may-care attitude to sex and drugs lie deep feelings regarding her parents' marriage break-up. She admits she uses Cook, sex and drugs to block out the pain and soon spirals further into self-destruction. This culminates with Effy's violent attack on Katie during a camping trip. Jealous that Freddie is now sexually involved with Katie, Effy gets high on magic mushrooms, sleeps with Freddie and, when Katie warns her to stay away from him, hits her with a rock.

Katie is hospitalised and the gang are furious with Effy, who goes on the run with Cook. In the final episode of series three, they track down Cook's drunken and useless father, and Effy worries about his bad influence on an already chaotic Cook. Calling upon Freddie and JJ for help, the gang take command of Cook's father's boat (by pushing him overboard) and sail back to Bristol.

In series four, Effy's mental state deteriorates further after her mother goes on an extended holiday. Home alone, she finally admits to Freddie that she loves him but, after they indulge in a drug-fuelled sexual marathon, Effy begins to behave in a terrifying way, pasting pictures of death all over her mother's bedroom and telling Freddie creatures are coming to get her. She freaks him out further by wanting to throw a 'goodbye' party for herself. During a street parade, filled with people dressed in demonic costumes, Effy loses her grip on reality completely, and becomes convinced that revellers are in fact demons trying to kill her. The gang become increasingly worried that Effy is suicidal. Their worst fears are confirmed when she is found on the bathroom floor with her wrists slashed.

Life takes an even more dramatic turn after Effy is admitted to a psychiatric hospital and her doctor, John Foster, becomes dangerously obsessed with her. While Effy is under hypnosis, Foster attempts to block out her memory and feelings for Freddie. Upon her release, Effy's

GLAMOROUS KAYA
PLAYS TROUBLED EFFY.

condition is very bad indeed – she has forgotten her friends and, worse, who she is. Effy tries to run away but is caught by Cook who helps her remember all she has forgotten. Finally, she tells him she loves Freddie. Cook accepts that, ultimately, Freddie and Effy belong together, and tells a confused and frightened Freddie not to give up on her. When Effy is re-admitted to hospital, Freddie is determined to keep her safe from Doctor Foster. After a confrontation, Foster appears to back off. The next day Foster invites Freddie to his home and viciously beats him to death with a baseball bat.

Still in hospital, and recovering well, Effy has no idea Freddie is dead – during a visit from Pandora and Katie, Effy says she thinks her illness has driven him away. After being released on Freddie's birthday, Effy heads to Freddie's shed where Cook finds her and helps her through her feelings of rejection by showing her Freddie's notebook. Reading it, she realises how much Freddie loves her. Despite Freddie's disappearance, the gang decide to hold a birthday party in his absence. In the *Skins* tradition of only featuring characters for two seasons, Effy's story ends there, comforted by her own knowledge of Freddie's love for her, and ignorant of his death.

Emily Fitch (played by Kathryn Prescott)

More sweet natured than her controlling older sister Katie, Emily is introduced in series three as one half of the Fitch twins. They catch Cook's eye on their first day at

Roundview, and he remarks to Emily that all boys 'love a bit a twin action, you could really make that work for you'. What he doesn't know is Emily is actually attracted to girls and struggling with romantic feelings towards her classmate Naomi. Emily has always felt in Katie's shadow and is desperate for some independence. She loves being a twin and knows that she shares a very special bond with Katie, but she is far less sexually experienced than her sister and is trying to find her own identity by wearing different clothes and hairstyles. We soon learn that – to Katie's horror – Emily and Naomi had shared a kiss during a drunken party before the gang began studying at Roundview. Katie is bitchy and cruel to Naomi, believing she seduced her sister with wicked lesbian wiles and for a while Emily goes along with this. She desperately wants to tell her sister the truth, but Katie apparently cannot stand the thought of Emily being gay and this causes Emily a great deal of torment.

Seeing Katie boss Emily around on their first morning at college, Effy remarks that Emily is the 'doormat'. This strengthens Emily's resolve to break free. Whilst Katie is busy eyeing up all the boys and telling everyone about her older, footballer boyfriend, Emily reveals that she has never been out with a boy. While a lot of the gang look surprised, Naomi does not, because she knows Emily's true sexuality.

The growing relationship between Emily and Naomi throughout series three is arguably one of the show's most tender love stories and drives their characters through most of series three and four. At first, Naomi tries to dismiss her feelings and keeps telling Emily she is straight. But Emily's strength of feeling drives her to keep trying to win Naomi's heart. They become friends and Emily helps Naomi with her campaign to run for college president until the two of them grow closer. On a day out to the countryside they eventually give in to their attraction for each other and, after a spot of skinny-dipping in the lake, they finally make love. Afterwards Naomi is confused and not ready to be upfront about her relationship with Emily. She leaves Emily in tears.

Emily seeks counselling to help her come to terms with her sexuality and Naomi's rejection, and to tell the truth about who she really is. She bumps into JJ as she is leaving the clinic – he's been having a medication assessment to help treat the symptoms of his autism. They go back to JJ's house and Emily reveals she is gay and JJ reveals he is a virgin. After comforting each other they end up having sex in order to both lose their virginity. By accident JJ blurts this out to Katie so, when Emily attempts to come out to her parents, Katie says that she can't be gay as she slept with JJ. She also tells Naomi to stay away from her sister. At the college ball, Katie corners Naomi again, but this time Emily won't stand for it. The two sisters come to blows with Emily wrestling Katie to the ground. Emily screams that she loves Naomi and that she wants to be with her. She explains that she will always love Katie but, despite being twins, they are different – Emily must be her own person.

At the beginning of series four, Emily is seen openly kissing Naomi in a nightclub – the two are now a couple.

Kathryn Prescott plays one half of the Fitch sisters, Emily.

The path of true love never runs smooth though — after a young girl called Sophia commits suicide at the club whilst high on MDMA, Emily becomes suspicious that Naomi knew her and may have had an affair with her. Naomi denies all knowledge of her but is covering up her guilt for having given Sophia the MDMA and for having had a brief, one-day fling with her behind Emily's back.

Emily discovers Naomi is lying and after a heart-to-heart with her father, who reveals that he once cheated on her mother, she appears to accept Naomi's betrayal. Soon though, her father reveals he is bankrupt and the whole Fitch family move into Naomi's house, much to the horror of Emily who is once again struggling with being cheated on.

During an impromptu barbecue, Emily becomes drunk, drugged and angry. She kisses another girl, throws Naomi in the paddling pool, lashes out at her mother (who refuses to accept her homosexuality) and has a fight with her sister. Emily can see no way to forgive Naomi until Naomi reveals that she has loved Katie since she was 12 years old. The romantic confession melts Emily's heart and they make up. They end the series happy and in love.

Known as the 'Naomily' storyline, many lesbian and gay groups supported the depiction of their relationship and it proved popular with lesbian viewers. In the US, a poll conducted by afterellen.com ranked Naomi and Emily as the top two fictional lesbian and bisexual characters of 2009.

F is for...

Family relationships

All the main characters have the sort of issues with their parents that are common among teenagers. Tony is a brilliant boy and much cleverer than his foul-mouthed father, who he deliberately provokes into fits of anger. Michelle loves her mother, but is exasperated by her relationships with numerous exploitive lovers. Jal's father is acrimoniously separated from her mother, and he blames Jal for being too like his estranged wife. Sid's father is a neurotic Scotsman who is always teetering on the edge of uncontrollable rage in reaction to Sid's disaster-prone ways. Maxxie's dad opposes his ambition to be a dancer and wants his son to join him in his building business. Anwar's mother and father are devout Muslims unhappy about

Anwar being influenced by his hedonistic friends. Chris's father has left home and his mother cannot cope with a teenage son. Cassie's self-obsessed parents have caused her host of mental problems.

Fans

Without its fans the show simply wouldn't exist. Every member of the cast and crew agrees that it is their fans that make *Skins* such a big hit. From its very first airing in 2007, *Skins* has been must-see viewing for millions of teenagers across the country. Fans have claimed that they have found it comforting to watch the show at difficult times in their lives because they could identify with the characters and their own problems: raging hormones, peer pressure, feelings of love and rejection, and the pressures of studying.

Facebook's *Skins* page has more than 2.5 million fans and numerous websites and forums have been set up for fans to chat, swap much-loved storylines and gossip about their favourite characters. E4 has established a strong link between the show and its fans through the official *Skins* websites. Characters regularly blog and reveal interesting facts about themselves as if they are real people and the lives the fans see on screen are actually happening.

The show's creator Bryan Elsey says, 'Our fans are incredibly loyal and full of integrity. They are our biggest critics and we listen to them.'

His son and co-creator Jamie Brittain reveals that some fans were disappointed when the whole cast were replaced at the end of series two. He said in an interview with Digital Spy, 'It was a decision we made because we wanted to look forward not back and reflect the two years students spend at sixth form college. Although it was a risk, it did work and we have done it again for series five and six.

'There are fans and then there are hardcore fans that are pretty hard to please because they want more of the old lot, but generally everyone has seemed to enjoy it. We communicate a lot with our fans, and listen to them, and read their comments and mail. Sometimes we use their ideas, sometimes we don't, but we have a level of interaction that I think is pretty unique.'

Film

Fans reacted with ecstatic cheers when it was announced in 2010 that *Skins* was to be made in a movie. The cast list was being kept tightly under wraps but insiders revealed that Nicholas Hoult and Dev Patel signed up to reprise their roles as Tony and Anwar. This is seen as a major coup – both actors have achieved Hollywood acclaim and should attract cinema goers who are not familiar with the TV show.

As it is tradition with *Skins* to replace the whole cast every two years, the movie will introduce a whole host of new characters to Roundview while re-introducing old and much-loved cast members.

The movie was shot in Bristol and was written by Jack Thorne, a regular *Skins* writer. He worked closely with the show's creator Bryan Elsley and director Charles Martin, another *Skins* regular.

Executive producer Steve Christian told reporters at a press conference: 'The biggest critics of *Skins* are the *Skins* fans. The programme has this incredible fan base, despite all the characters changing, and they will not accept anything that is not first rate.'

Hoping to attract an older audience to the movie as well as the teenage target audience he revealed he knows full well that it has become something of a guilty please for older, curious viewers.

'Look, I'm a middle- aged bloke with two kids, I should hate *Skins* but I absolutely love it,' adds Christian. 'And then I talk to my mates, people not in the film industry, and it's the same thing – they watch it and they love it and it's all down to the quality of the production.'

First Episode

For anyone expecting a cosy teenage saga of lovable youngsters enjoying their carefree teens, the first episode of *Skins*, created by father-and-son team of writers Bryan Elsley and Jamie Brittain, exploded on our screens with the impact of a ten-car motorway pile up.

Centring on the intimate lives of a group of Bristol teenagers attending the fictional Roundview Sixth Form College, we knew we were in for something different when we saw Sid's morning masturbation interrupted by a mobile call from his best friend Tony, who immediately

SOME OF THE ORIGINAL CAST OF *SKINS*: MIKE BAILEY (SID), LARISSA WILSON (JAL), HANNAH MURRAY (CASSIE) AND DEV PATEL (ANWAR).

demonstrated his manipulative abilities by telling Sid his plan for the day: to get Sid to lose his virginity.

In the fast-paced scenes – starting at breakfast time – we meet Tony's foul-mouthed father (played by Harry Enfield), his long suffering mother, and Effy, Tony's wild younger sister. Effy returns from an obviously torrid night on the tiles to be secretly let into the house by Tony.

Tony's plan for the evening is that his group of friends will attend a party given by Abigail, a pupil at a posh private school, where Tony had been co-opted into the choir. Sid will buy an ounce of spliff from a local drug dealer, who operates his business from a suburban brothel. Tony and Sid will sell the drugs to other partygoers, keeping enough for their own consumption, and get a girl 'spliffed up' so that Sid can lose his virginity with her.

In the course of the day, we meet the rest of the gang. Maxxie, a gay, gifted tap-dancer; Anwar, Maxxie's straight best friend and a Muslim who we first see praying, despite his attraction to his close companion's hedonistic ways. We also meet Jal, a clever black girl whose psychology essay on relationships moves their teacher, Angie, to break down in tears because she had broken up with her fiancé. Her distress is painful to Chris, another of the gang, who is besotted with Angie. After class he comforts her.

Meanwhile, Sid – in his own words 'a total fuck-up' – goes to the ornate suburban brothel, where the scantily clad workers entertain him while he waits for a drug dealer known as the 'Mad Twatter'. On arrival, it is clear the Mad Twatter – who sports a lavish handlebar moustache – is insane. He explains his exorbitant monetary arrangements to Sid – who wants to buy on credit – and threatens to cut off Sid's balls if he reneges on the deal.

Maxxie, Anwar and Chris decline Tony's invitation to the party because Maxxie tells them of a Big Gay Night Out, an event that promises to be much more fun than a posh girl's party. Tony arrives at the party with Michelle, his stunning girlfriend, and another member of the gang. Michelle has brought her friend Cassie, with whom it is planned Sid will lose his virginity. Cassie is a beautiful blonde anorexic who has just been discharged from hospital after a suicide attempt. She is already happily medicated up to her eyeballs and seems pleased with the prospect of sleeping with someone she has never met before. Sid arrives with a huge bundle of spliff that Mad Twatter has forced him to take. The party is underway, but it is more sedate than expected.

The Big Gay Night Out has proved to be a flop, so Maxxie, Anwar and Chris turn up to the posh girl's party and liven things up.

Sid spends time with Cassie, who casually offers him sex, but says he must be quick, as she has taken a 'shit load' of pills. She passes out and – thinking she has taken an overdose – the gang drives her to hospital. On arrival she wakes up and the gang somehow contrive to drive the car they have 'borrowed' into the river.

The rawness of the language, the explicit sexual behaviour and nudity in the first episode brought a storm of controversy down on the programme and its

DAKOTA BLUE RICHARDS.

creators as well as strong critical reactions, both approving and disapproving.

But *Skins* had the last laugh. It attracted a record 1.65 million viewers, spawned numerous fan forums and the younger generation just couldn't get enough of it.

Franky Fitzgerald (played by Dakota Blue Richards)

Making a late entrance at Roundview College, and causing one hell of a stir in series five, is Franky. Thanks to her unconventional fashion choices (she greases back her hair, wears men's three-piece suits and spats shoes), androgynous Franky is at first viewed as a freak by the hip mainstream students.

Franky's past is a bit of a mystery, but it soon becomes clear why she has started Roundview late. She has transferred from another college where she was the victim of a vicious bullying campaign.

Her childhood is shrouded in secrecy – all we know is that she was adopted by gay couple Geoff and Jeff and refers to them as Dad and Dad. Quiet and reserved, Franky spends a lot of time at home alone and is a talented filmmaker, producing animation shorts on her home computer.

It seems that history is about to repeat itself when she falls foul of Mini McGuiness, the college's queen bee. Popular but insecure, Mini takes an instant dislike to Franky and sets about making her life a misery. Mini's friends Grace and Liv feel she is being unfair and want to befriend Franky, as do farmer's son Alo and metalhead Rich, who are also unconventional and looking to make new friends.

Liv and Grace persuade Mini to give Franky a chance. They take her shopping and they show her how to wear make-up – Mini desperately tries to change Franky's look and forces her to buy a sexy, sequinned dress for Mini's upcoming party. Later, they visit Franky's house and Mini sees bullying comments and horrible pictures of Franky that have been posted on her page of a social networking site. One of Franky's dads discovers Mini looking and tells her to leave – revealing that Franky had a terrible time at her last college and that he couldn't bear for her to go through it again.

The next day, Franky arrives at college to find that Mini has got her boyfriend Nick to paste the pictures on the walls of the college corridor. Franky is devastated. After receiving some brutally bitchy comments from Mini, Franky runs to a secluded area outside the city and shoots at an abandoned fridge with an air pistol. Distressed and crying, Franky suddenly realises she is being watched by a mysterious, handsome boy her own age. Without revealing who he is he tells her she is beautiful. When she denies this he says, 'Then why do I see a fucking glorious head-fuck then?'

Empowered, Franky decides to take on Mini. She does not realise that the kind stranger is Matty, the black sheep brother of Nick, Mini's sporting hero boyfriend.

The second and third generation of *Skins* enjoying their moments in the spotlight!

Above: The second generation: Kathryn Prescott (Emily), Klariza Clayton (Karen, Freddie's sister), Luke Pasqualino (Freddie), Ollie Barbeiri (JJ), Lisa Blackwell (Pandora), Megan Prescott (Katie) and Kaya Scodelario (Effy).

Below:The third generation: Alexander Arnold (Rich), Laya Lewis (Liv), Freya Mavor (Mini) and Sean Teale (Nick).

Childhood Stars!

Above left: A grown-up Nicholas (Tony)!

Above right: Dakota plays Franky Fitzgerald, a clever but reticent teenage girl.

Below left: On the red carpet for the premiere of *About a Boy* with Hugh Grant and Victoria Smurfit. Acting came very naturally to Nicholas!

Below right: Dakota was already an established star before joining *Skins*.

The gorgeous Dev Patel went on to become an international movie star after finishing *Skins*.

Joe Dempsie played one of the most popular characters in *Skins*, lovable and troubled Chris.

Skins have had a string of famous people star in the show!

Above left: Harry Enfield plays Jim Stonem, Tony and Effy's father. He appears in the first three series and even directed some of the episodes!

Above right: As Pandora's mother Angela, Sally Phillips gives a hilarious performance of a seemingly straight-laced parent who enjoys S and M sex on the side!

Below left: David Baddiel's character has an affair with Effy's mum, who just happens to be his partner in real life – Morwenna Banks!

Below right: Arabella Weir plays Michelle's mum, but she is best known for her role in *The Fast Show*.

The beautiful Kaya Scodelario (Effy).

Luke Pasqualino played Freddie Mclair in series three and four.
Characters Effy and Freddie had a difficult relationship.

Above: Hannah Murray (Cassie) and Mike Bailey (Sid) were part of the original cast of *Skins*.

Below: Double Trouble! Real life twins Kathryn and Megan (the Fitch sisters) had a lot to live up to as part of the second generation of *Skins*.

After many trials and tribulations in the first two episodes, Franky and Mini eventually find peace with each other. When Mini's sad home life and insecurities are revealed and her friends turn against her, it is Franky that comforts her and Mini realises how stupid she has been.

Freddie McLair (played by Luke Pasqualino)

Freddie kicks off series three with a thrilling skateboard ride through the streets of Bristol. Effortlessly cool, brooding, tall, dark and handsome, Freddie is more laid back than JJ and Cook, his two best friends since primary school. They are the self-styled Three Musketeers and begin college believing they will always be the closest of friends. But then Effy comes along.

Freddie is instantly attracted to the mysterious and beautiful Effy, but so are his two best friends. Effy certainly gives him the eye but, before the first episode is out, she is having sex with Cook. This sets them all on a path of heartbreak, rejection and unrequited love.

Freddie, who is often seen sporting unexplained cuts and bruises, a reference to his skateboarding, is still trying to come to terms with the recent death of his mother. He lives with his dad Leo and sister Karen and often retreats to his shed to smoke weed, contemplate life and look at pornography away from his sister's and dad's radar. The shed is decorated with graffiti and old armchairs and has long been the official headquarters of the Three

LUKE PASQUALINO PLAYS THE EFFORTLESSLY COOL AND ATTRACTIVE FREDDIE.

Musketeers, where the boys have been meeting since they were kids.

Unlike Cook, Freddie is sensitive and not promiscuous, and he has begun to tire of Cook's wild and unpredictable ways. On Cook's 17th birthday, Cook persuades the gang to gatecrash an engagement party Freddie's sister Karen is attending. Cook gets out of control and ends up fighting with the girl's father, local gangster Jonnie White. Freddie tells Cook he cannot look after him anymore and their relationship becomes increasingly strained, with JJ in the middle, trying to keep the peace.

Freddie is also struggling at home, becoming distant from his Dad and sister. Karen is obsessed with winning an *X Factor*-style show and, much to Freddie's disgust, is using the death of their mother to win sympathy votes. His father tells him he should support his sister and it is what his mother would have wanted. But when his father redecorates the shed and turns it into a rehearsal dance studio for Karen, Freddie is furious at having lost his place of refuge.

Freddie pines for Effy throughout series three. There are occasional tender moments between them, and they share the odd kiss, but Effy continuously rejects him. When he tells her he loves her, Effy tells Freddie she will break his heart. Knowing that Effy doesn't love Cook but continues to sleep with him drives Freddie mad – he falls into a relationship with Katie, one of the twins, to try and get over her. When Cook inadvertently takes some of JJ's medication, it compels him to tell the truth and he reveals that he is in love with Effy. Freddie, although still angry and distant from Cook, understands the pain of loving Effy and when she says that she doesn't love Cook back, it gives Freddie reason to hope that they can be together.

Katie becomes very possessive of Freddie and tries to flaunt their relationship in front of Effy at every opportunity. When the group take a camping trip, Effy and Freddie sneak off and have sex together after they have taken magic mushrooms.

Suspicious, Katie attacks Effy and tells her to stay away from her man. But Effy is high on a 'bad trip' and hits Katie with a rock. The gang look for Katie in the morning, but Effy does not reveal their fight. Freddie is disgusted with Effy when he finds out that Katie was left unconscious in the woods all night and is now hospitalised. Effy flees town.

The final episode of series three sees Effy and Cook on the run. Effy calls Freddie and asks him to help Cook, who is increasingly in the grip of his drunken father. Freddie says, 'Why can't you help him?' Effy replies, 'Because I love you.'

Series four begins with the ongoing love triangle but – after Cook is imprisoned for lashing out at a fellow party goer when he sees Freddie and Effy kiss – Effy finally tells Cook she loves Freddie.

Although madly in love, Effy and Freddie embark on a hedonistic marathon of sex and drugs and life takes a dramatic downturn for Freddie as his college work and friendships begin to suffer. Freddie is threatened with expulsion unless he starts to do better at college and Effy behaves in increasingly erratic and psychotic ways. It is revealed that Freddie's mother also suffered from psychotic depression and had committed suicide. Freddie blames his father for not doing enough to help his mother and pledges to help Effy through her illness.

Effy's condition worsens to the point that she slashes her wrists in a toilet. Freddie feels her cannot help her and tells her mother that Effy needs her, not him. But Cook tells Freddie not to give up on her. Effy soon falls under the spell of psychiatrist Dr Foster, who develops a dangerous obsession with her. Hypnotised into forgetting who she loves, Effy once more spurns Freddie.

Effy is released from hospital but, when she is readmitted after a relapse, Freddie confronts Dr Foster and tells him to stay away from her. The doctor agrees and the next day invites Freddie to his home to discuss the situation. Without telling anyone Freddie goes to his house only to find Foster wielding a baseball bat. In a particularly vicious scene, Foster beats Freddie to death.

Freddie's killing was greeted with horror by fans of the show. Blogs and forums were full of posts by fans who revealed their shattered emotions, shock and terror at the death of a beloved character, with some even writing that they couldn't sleep after viewing the episode. The *Sun* ran a story claiming that *Skins* fans intended to boycott the rest of the show in revenge for the creators killing Freddie off.

ACTING RUNS IN FREYA MAVOR'S FAMILY SO PLAYING MINI COMES NATURALLY TO HER.

Freya Mavor (plays Mini McGuiness)

With long legs, long blonde hair and a long list of admirers, the beautiful Scots schoolgirl looks every inch the new Roundview queen bee in the latest season of *Skins*. Chosen from 8000 hopefuls at the open auditions, Freya, who had no formal acting experience before taking the role, still can't quite believe she is starring in a show that she has been a fan of for years. 'I remember receiving the phone call to say I'd got the part,' she says. 'I couldn't stop laughing. I was thinking: What just happened?'

Freya is still at school and has to fit her studies around her *Skins* shooting schedule – she missed the deadline to apply to university because she was busy filming *Skins*. 'That really sucks,' she says. 'I was hoping to apply for a deferred entry to study philosophy combined with theatre studies but this has been the opportunity of a lifetime and there was no way I was going to miss out on playing Mini.'

More experienced cast members Clare Grogan and Kelly Brook – who both make guest appearances in series five – have tipped Freya as an actress going places and believe this will be a stepping stone to a very successful drama career.

After all, the theatre does run in her family. Freya's dad, James Mavor, is an award-winning playwright who heads up the MA screenwriting course at Napier University and her grandfather Ronald Bingo Mavor was *The Scotsman*'s theatre critic in the early 1960s. He went on to become the director of the Scottish Arts Council. And Freya's great-grandfather, playwright Oswald Henry Mavor, helped to set up Glasgow's Citizens Theatre.

Freya is still pinching herself for being on TV at all and reveals she has got some stick at school – mainly from boys – about the show's sexual content. In an interview with *The Scotsman* she said: 'Everyone at school has an opinion on *Skins* because they all watch it,' she says. 'It was exactly like that before I was in it. I remember going to school and everyone saying, "Did you see what happened on *Skins* last night?" It's a show that causes a lot of debate between people my age.'

As a member of the third generation of cast members, Freya has grown up watching *Skins* and often found the show mirrored her own life. 'I remember so many times hearing friends saying, "This feels like such a *Skins* moment". That's almost become like a defining thing, when something's really, really extreme, when you have a crazy bizarre random night.

'Once I was running down a massive hill with two friends at 5am and the sun was coming up and we had to get to this party. I really felt I was in the show then.'

Freya has been kept very busy since her debut as Mini and was given the role of Kate Middleton in the TV movie *Kate and Wills*, which aired just after the Royal Wedding. Sticking to her Scottish roots, she has also modelled for Pringle.

G is for...

Grace Violet (played by Jessica Sula)

The most sweet and loveable member of the third generation is Grace. Living up to her name, she is graceful, elegant and loves ballet. Her idols are Audrey Hepburn and Grace Kelly and she tries to emulate their sophisticated fashions. But there is a lot more to Grace than meets the eye. Part of Mini's gang, she's also quite a skilful shoplifter with a talent for using her innocent looks as a ploy to avoid detection.

At first, Grace seems fluffy, silly and under Mini's thumb, but we soon realise she is ready to break out on her own and play Mini at her own game. Grace immediately likes new girl Franky, and stands up for her when Mini starts her bullying. Enlisting the help of Alo and Rich,

Grace makes Franky feel more welcome in Bristol and helps her join the gang. Eventually, Mini backs down and they also become friends.

Despite their apparent differences, Grace is also attracted to metalhead Rich. At first he thinks her attentions are silly but after she shakes off her goody two shoes image and dresses in leather and a dog collar, he sees past the girlie image and realises she is made of very interesting stuff.

Life has been quite simple for Grace for a long time but during her first year at Roundview her naivety is shattered. Jessica Sula who plays Grace says in an interview with the *Sun*: 'She's a romantic. She likes to think she's not aware of issues going on around her. She likes to block them out and believe that everything is a fairytale fantasy world. But soon she is dealing with some fairly serious issues.

'But she also brings a light-heartedness and she is kind to everyone, so I think she is a bridge builder. She will try and fix things. It's always nice to have that because that type of person relaxes you if you're in an awkward situation.'

Guest Stars

From the outset, *Skins* attracted a host of established and much-loved British actors and comedians to small cameo roles in the show. While most of the main characters were made up of inexperienced unknowns, the roles of older generation characters such as parents and teachers had famous British stars queuing up to get in on the act. They added a certain gravitas to a show that relied on youngsters whom no one had heard of. It all started with Harry Enfield, who plays Tony and Effy Stonem's dad, and is a friend of creator Bryan Elsey.

Co-creator Jamie Brittain, who is also Elsey's son explained to Digital Spy, 'Dad asked Harry as a favour to come and be on the show and once we got him a lot of other people were, like, "Oh, this could be quite a fun thing to do," so we got lots of great people. Sometimes we hear about people who really want to be in the show; other times, we just ask people and they say yes.'

'I was at an awards ceremony and I met the actor Chris Addison, who's in *The Thick of It*, and I said, 'Do you want to be in *Skins*?' and he said yes. So I said I'd write him a part. Sometimes you just meet people like that and so we find a part for them.'

Other famous actors to appear on the show include: Maureen Lipman, Will Young, Shane Ritchie, Mackenzie Crook and Pauline Quirke.

H is for...

Harry Enfield (plays Jim Stonem, Tony and Effy's father)

Harry Enfield, playing Jim Stonem, Tony and Effy's father, appears in the first three series and directed some of the episodes in series two and three. Jim Stonem finds life difficult – he can't understand why his wife is so bored and his children baffle him. Tony treats his dad with good-natured contempt and Effy barely acknowledges his existence. Jim responds to even the simplest problems in life with a constant barrage of foul-mouthed invective, so is utterly shattered when he discovers his wife has had an affair with his boss. There's not much to Jim Stonem's character, but Harry Enfield is such a brilliant actor he manages to make a fairly two-dimensional part come alive.

A comedian, actor, writer, and director. Enfield read politics at the University of York, where he met Bryan Elsley, a fellow student, who went on to create *Skins* with his son Jamie Brittain.

Homophobia

There are scenes depicting homophobia in the first and second series. Maxxie is taunted and threatened by a gang of yobs who live on his council estate. Maxxie is unperturbed by the menacing youths but when an incident looks as if it may turn to violence, Maxxie's father (played by Bill Bailey) appears and frightens the daylights out of the gang leader.

Anwar is also unsettled by Maxxie's sexual orientation, mainly because he imagines his Muslim family would be appalled by him keeping company with someone who is gay. But Anwar's father has a conversation with Maxxie at Anwar's 17th birthday party, in which he obliquely acknowledges Maxxie's homosexuality and condones his son's friendship.

Emily in series two is a lesbian but her twin sister Katie is homophobic. In series five, Franky is called a freak for dressing like a man and for having two adoptive gay dads.

Hugo Speer (plays Dr John Foster)

Playing the doctor who turns murderer was a far cry from Speer's most memorable role as the hugely well-endowed

HUGO SPEER PLAYS THE EVIL MURDERER DR JOHN FOSTER.

stripper in *The Full Monty.* Fans reacted with outrage when Foster beat Freddie to death with a baseball bat and Speer's performance was rated terrifying and haunting on websites.

Speer, 41, had an impressive career behind him before taking his part on *Skins.* He began his acting career appearing in TV series *The Bill* and *Heartbeat,* and played a minor role in the film *Bhaji on the Beach* before his first notable appearance as Guy in *The Full Monty.*

Hollywood beckoned and Speer starred alongside Oscar winner Nicole Kidman to play her brother in *The Interpreter.* He is currently starring as Warren in the paranormal Sky TV drama *Bedlam.*

Revealing that his dark role in *Skins* paved the way for more chilling roles Speer told the *Sun* newspaper, '*Skins* was way leftfield for me, playing a loving and sensitive man who suddenly beats a teenager to death. I got a bit of stick for killing Freddie, who was the most popular good-looking actor in the series! It's great to be given those types of roles though.'

I is for...

Influences

Although the idea for *Skins* originally came from scriptwriter Bryan Elsey, when he read the first draft of the script to his teenage son Jamie Brittain, Jamie described it as a load of middle-aged bollocks. Elsey brought Jamie onboard to help him write a credible script and it was his experiences of being a teenager in today's world that hugely influenced the show. Jamie revealed in an interview with online entertainment magazine Pressplus 1:

If I'm honest, the characters in *Skins* are mostly based on mine and my little sister's experiences. I can't speak for anywhere else, but being a teenager in Bristol in the Noughties was a lot of fun. Teenagers were liberated beings with complex and varied social and emotional lives. Bryan and I came up with a bunch of characters based on me and my sister's friends. We started with archetypes, and the complication and nuance came later. By series three we had got much better at it and wanted to create complicated characters from the off. But having said that, even though they were based on people I knew the characters flew away from these origins pretty quickly. Take Tony for instance. He was based on one of my best mates. He had the body, the intellect, strength and depth of him but none of his cruelness or malice.

They also drew on popular US dramas that Jamie had been watching as a kid and cite the original *90210*, *Buffy the Vampire Slayer*, *Dawson's Creek* and *The OC* as influences on *Skins*.

J is for...

Jack O'Connell (Plays James Cook)

Jack had already starred in the controversial, cult movie *This is England* when he took the role of James Cook in series three and four.

Having been at the same drama workshop as Joe Dempsie, who played Chris in the original series, Jack was drawn to auditioning for *Skins*. In an interview with Sky TV Jack said, 'When I found out they were completely recasting for the second generation I couldn't let the opportunity go. The show is so cleverly written. They've managed to hit this reality which kept me interested.

'Not only that, I got to do what loads of young blokes want to do all the time and I got paid for it. They call this work apparently. On *Skins* every day can potentially be

JACK O'CONNELL (CENTRE)
WITH CO-STARS OLLIE AND LILY.

the most exciting day of your life. All the nakedness, all the sex scenes. I could have been doing a lot worse. I'm very grateful.'

Skins co-creator Jamie Brittain says the moment he met O'Connell he knew he had to have him as Cook. 'The charisma and energy he had was so compelling. There was no-one else who could play him in my mind.'

Chris won a TV Choice Best Actor award for his role as Cook and since leaving the show has been busy with TV and film work. In July 2010, O'Connell starred in *Dive*, a major two-part drama for BBC2, where a young teenage couple must come to terms with an unexpected pregnancy. His depiction of Robert was described by *The Observer* reviewer Euan Ferguson as 'a performance that is of an actor twice his years: mesmerising, comedic and soulful.'

Cook was a complicated and controversial role but was one of *Skins* best-loved characters.

Jal Fazer (played by Larissa Wilson)

Jal is different to the rest of the gang in series one and two. She is an extremely clever and highly gifted classical clarinettist. Her father, Ronny Fazer, is a famous and retired hip hop artist, which makes her family far richer than those of her friends. She has two brothers, Ace and Lynton, who – despite their wealthy middle-class advantages and much to Jay's contempt – constantly attempt to give the impression of being ghetto kids.

Jal's mother has left her father and this causes tension between father and daughter, especially because Jal is so like her mother.

Jal is the most mature of the Roundview College gang, and her occasional exasperation with her friends is usually caused by their comparatively childish behaviour. She is uninterested in clothes, but her best friends are Michelle – who is always dressed in the height of fashion – and Chris, the least mature of the whole gang.

An intellectual and gifted teenager, Jal does not fit into the mould. Jal's disillusion with the system is heightened by the attitude of the head teacher of Roundview College. She is aware that Jal has hopes of becoming the BBC Young Musician of the Year, but instead of being proud of this achievement, the head is more interested in using Jal's potential fame as a way of boosting the school's reputation and attracting future funding.

Jal has high expectations of her friends and is made angry by Tony's shabby treatment of Michelle and by Sid's indifference to Cassie's affection. Her principles often make her seem something of a goody-goody and it is sometimes pointed out by others that she puts her music before human relationships – in Chris's words, 'you don't have sex, you have clarinet lessons'. Eventually, Jal and Chris make a pact that she will stop saying 'no' to everything and he will give up his 'don't give a fuck' attitude to life.

According to her fictional *Skins* page, Jal despises modern pop artists, saying she wants to 'sue MTV for prolonged emotional distress'. She likes eating chips,

Maxxie's dancing, and the relationship between maths and music (Pythagorean triples).

Jal is aware that Chris has a growing addiction to drugs, and she grows closer to Chris when he is abandoned by his mother and left homeless. She is further angered by Sid's treatment of Cassie – she takes her to hospital after an overdose and tells the doctors that she is Cassie's sister. She dismisses Sid from the hospital. Later, at Anwar's birthday party, Chris starts a brawl and Jal shows her prowess in fighting much larger male opponents. Finally, at a party, Jal shows her wilder side when Chris dares her to go and get the hat of the singer with the band. Uncharacteristically, she downs a can of beer and passionately kisses the singer on stage as she takes his hat. Inevitably, Chris and Jal end up getting together and Chris realises he is over Angie. However, Jal falls pregnant and not knowing whether to keep the baby or not she keeps it quiet from Chris. Jal continues to struggle with the decisions she needs to make. While she agonises over whether or not to tell Chris she is pregnant, it is intimated that Chris has a secret of his own.

Jal goes for an audition at a prestigious college of arts. The examiners are dismissive of her choice of music, claiming it is the easiest piece. Defiantly, Jal changes to the most difficult piece and performs brilliantly. But, when she returns home, she finds an anxious Cassie sitting on the table in the apartment who has come to tell her that Chris has suffered a stroke and has the same hereditary illness that caused the brain haemorrhages that killed his brother.

Chris recovers only to be told by Jal that she is pregnant

Larissa and Mike Bailey at the BAFTAs in 2008.

and intends to abort their child. Cassie tries to cheer him up by stealing him a t-shirt but he wants to talk about Jal. After a short while, he realises he can't remember her name any more and knows he is suffering a second stroke. A distraught Cassie calls an ambulance but it is too late. Chris dies in her arms.

A devastated Jal goes ahead with the abortion and she can barely face getting out of bed on the day of Chris's funeral. However, she turns up to watch it from afar (the gang have been banned from attending by Chris's dad) and makes a moving speech. The gang set off fireworks then disperse, leaving a crying Jal sitting by Chris's grave. Chris's dad approaches and offers his comfort and sympathies.

Although devastated by Chris's death at the end of series two, the gang meet up to open each other's A Level results. It is revealed Jal has done extremely well passing with two As and one B and the viewer is left knowing that life will eventually be good again for Jal.

Jessica Sula (Plays Grace Blood)

It came as somewhat of a relief to Jessica that her role in *Skins* was going to be sweet, caring and dreamy – quite a departure from the sexually experienced, rebellious girls usually found in the program. Jessica was a bit apprehensive about taking a role in the show because of its sexy reputation, and she admits that when she told her mum about the job she looked horrified.

The show's producers decided that the fifth series would

be lighter, more fun and sillier than the previous series but Jessica, who was aged just 16 when she made her *Skins* debut, knew that eventually she would be doing risqué scenes in *Skins* too.

Born in Swansea, South Wales, Jessica – like her on-screen character – is studying for her A Levels at sixth form college. It took seven rounds of the auditioning process before Jessica won the role of ballet dancing Grace and she admits that when she saw how long the queue was for the first audition she nearly gave up. Aside from school plays and youth theatre this is her first chance at proper acting.

'In the end I queued for five and half hours, she recalls, 'but thank God, because I am thrilled to be in the show.'

Amusingly, Jessica almost got arrested during filming. During a scene where Grace pinches some make-up from a shop, she has to run out of the shop and shout 'leg it' to her mates. The scene was filmed in the busy Bristol Cabot Shopping Centre at midday and a real-life policeman started chasing her, believing she was pinching the makeup for real.

Joe Dempsie (played Chris Miles)

Since appearing as Chris in the very first series of *Skins*, Joe has notched up an impressive amount of work. In an episode of the fourth series of *Doctor Who*, 'The Doctor's Daughter' Joe played the role of a young soldier. In 2009 he appeared as Duncan McKenzie in 'The Damned

JOE DEMPSIE FULLY CLOTHED! UNLIKE HIS CHARACTER CHRIS WHO WAS THE FIRST OF THE CAST TO APPEAR FULLY NAKED IN *SKINS*.

United' alongside Michael Sheen, Jim Broadbent, Stephen Graham and Timothy Spall.

Joe was noted for appearing totally naked in *Skins*, and for being the very first character to be killed off. It seems to have enhanced his career though and he has a lot of work lined up for the future. Joe received his training at the Central Junior Television Workshop, Nottingham alongside fellow *Skins* actor Jack O'Connell who plays Cook.

Early in his career he took parts in the television series *Doctors*, *Peak Practice*, *Sweet Medicine* and *Born and Bred* as well as the films *One for the Road* and *Heartlands*. He was also in *The Tony Martin Story*, a BBC documentary-drama about Norfolk farmer Tony Martin who was imprisoned after shooting an intruder, an incident which caused national headlines.

Joe was born in Liverpool in 1987 but he grew up in West Bridgford, Nottinghamshire. He is a keen Nottingham Forest fan and attends as many home and away matches as he can manage.

John Sessions (plays Jeff, one of Franky's gay dads)

In yet another genius *Skins* guest star guise is John Sessions, playing one of Franky's Territorial Army-obsessed gay dads.

His film work includes *The Sender, The Bounty*, and *Castaway* and he was well known for his hilarious turns as a regular panellist on the improvisation show *Whose*

JOHN SESSIONS.

Line is it Anyway? Sessions also has an impressive Shakespearean background. His most recent television appearance was as Donovan Credo, the hotel owner in the TV series *Hotel Babylon*.

Jonah 'JJ' Jones (played by Ollie Barbieri)

From the moment we see JJ, we know he is sweet, kind, vulnerable and about to get the shock of his life when he joins Roundview. Making friends with large groups of people is a challenge for JJ, who has autism, a condition which can make social interaction difficult.

JJ is best friends with Freddie and Cook and they are very protective of him. Above average intelligence and very articulate, JJ excels at maths and science although he requires medication to help regulate his short temper and 'rages' which are a symptom of his condition.

He is one of the most likeable and amusing members of the gang and uses magic tricks to help him overcome his awkwardness with new people and his habit for saying inappropriate things and blurting out the truth at inconvenient moments. JJ is also fascinated by astronomy, plays the ukulele and is very close to his mum.

JJ finds himself caught up in the Freddie-Effy-Cook love triangle and, although he is attracted to Effy himself, he becomes increasingly frustrated over her influence on his two closest friends. With Freddie prone to withdrawing into himself, JJ is forced to spend more time with Cook,

KAYA AND OLLIE
ENJOYING TIME
AWAY FROM FILMING
SKINS AT THE UK
PREMIER OF
MARLEY AND ME.

whose desire to help his friend lose his virginity involves taking him to a seedy brothel.

JJ is terrified and asks the prostitute if they can just kiss. Although he's frustrated at never having a girlfriend he is too sensitive to lose his virginity to just anyone. Nevertheless, Cook laughs at him and calls him a 'pussy' for just kissing. Cook and JJ's relationship is an incongruous one but adds depth to Cook's character – Cook would never hurt JJ deliberately and would defend him to the grave.

In the episode 'JJ', which concentrates on his character, we learn more about his life with autism. He struggles to tell his friends how he really feels, and wants them to stop ruffling his hair and treat him as a grown-up. He wants his mum to stop worrying about him so much and he wants his friends to sort out the Effy situation so he doesn't have to choose between Freddie and Cook. But most of all he wants to feel 'normal'.

At a meeting with his apparently uninterested doctor, JJ is prescribed his usual medication along with an additional prescription for 'Stun'. Upon leaving the clinic, he bumps into Emily who tells him she has been seeing a counsellor and that she has also been prescribed Stun. Emily has been seeking help about coming out as gay and reveals her secret to JJ. In return, he confides in Emily and tells her that he is also struggling with being a virgin. As the two bond further, Emily reveals how hurt she is about Naomi's confusing attitude to their relationship. JJ and Emily end up agreeing to have sex to help Emily to feel in control and so

JJ can finally lose his virginity. Emily describes the situation as a 'one time charity event'.

The writers often use JJ's habit of blurting out the truth as a device for characters to find out what is going on. JJ inadvertently reveals that Cook has been sleeping with Pandora thus hurting Thomas, her boyfriend. He also lets it slip to Katie that her sister Emily is gay, and then tells Freddie he had sex with Emily (who then reveals it to Katie, enabling her to hurt Naomi). Without the character of JJ it would have been much harder for those secrets to get out.

JJ gets closer to Thomas in series four. This highlights his growing maturity and ability to make new friends. He becomes attracted to a single mum Lara but, after a series of unfortunate events (which include Cook giving him disastrous dating advice, run-ins with the father of Lara's son Albert, and JJ's mum calling Lara a slut through a Freudian slip), Lara dumps him.

Heartbroken, JJ recruits the local ukulele band and serenades Lara with a surprisingly good rendition of Spandau Ballet's *True* to win her over again. Although we do not see Lara again for the rest of the series, JJ is often seen bouncing baby Albert on his knee which indicates they are still together and that Lara trusts JJ to look after her little boy. By the end of series four, JJ seems far happier and much more comfortable with himself.

The producers and creators of *Skins* were very careful about how they depicted JJ's autism. They wanted to create a character that would give truth to his condition without defining him. It was important to the creators to show how autism affected JJ's life, while also showing there was much more to him than his autistic traits.

Writer Jamie Brittain reveals, 'I am very proud of JJ. We worked for ages, months really, working him out and where he would go. I was very pleased with the result.'

JJ's episode brought in 997,000 viewers and was E4's highest-rated programme of the week with an audience share of 4.8 percent. However, it drew criticism from the gay community for depicting lesbian Emily having 'charity sex' with JJ.

Jonny White (played by Mackenzie Crook)

Jonny White is a psychopathic local gangster. He deals in drugs and is an illegal slum landlord. Thomas, an innocent newcomer from the Congo, falls foul of White when he is found squatting in one of his flats. White demands an exorbitant sum that Thomas must produce in a few days. To get the money Thomas decides to deal in the home grown cannabis Pandora's aunt grows, but he doesn't realise he is dealing in one of White's clubs. Meanwhile, Cook takes the gang to crash an expensive party on a private boat. It turns out to be an engagement party for Jonny White's daughter and the son of a rival gang. The two gangs are attending the event in force, as the wedding is intended to seal a peace treaty between them and usher in a new era of criminal cooperation. Cook's drinking and drug taking induces fearless behaviour and he shows a lack of respect towards

MACKENZIE CROOK PLAYS PSYCHOPATH GANGSTER JONNY WHITE.

Jonny White that leads to a fight between the rival gangs and ruins the peace treaty. Cook escapes unharmed, and later takes JJ to a brothel where they discover Jonny White chained up for sado-masochistic sex with a prostitute. Cook tortures the helpless Jonny White, who vows he will kill Cook when next they meet.

To make peace between the two gangs, Thomas eventually challenges Jonny White to a trial of strength. White, who earlier demonstrated his ability to drink a pot of boiling pot noodles, chooses to make the trial a chili pepper eating contest. But he is no match for Thomas, who has been raised eating the fiery peppers his mother grew in her garden. Thomas triumphs and Jonny White is humiliated so he backs down and never causes the gang trouble again.

Josie Lawrence (plays Liz, Sid's mum)

Josie Lawrence is a comedienne and actress who first came to prominence through her work with the Comedy Store Players improvisational troupe and the television series *Whose Line Is It Anyway?* She also played Manda Best, Minty's girlfriend, in *EastEnders.*

Lawrence holds a bachelor of arts honours degree from Dartington College of Arts. From 1994 – 1996 Lawrence took the lead as Katharine in the Royal Shakespeare Company production of *The Taming of the Shrew* in both Stratford-upon-Avon and London. Her performance earned her the Dame Peggy Ashcroft award for Best

Actress. She also appeared in *Faust* and *The Cherry Orchard*. She later starred at Shakespeare's Globe as Benedick in an all-female production of *Much Ado About Nothing*. A gifted singer, Josie took the lead role of Anna in the stage musical *The King and I*. She also spent eight months in 2003 walking across China, Cuba, Peru and Tanzania for Breakthrough Breast Cancer. She is single and lives in London with her two cats. Josie's *Skins* character Liz is unhappily married and sexually frustrated. Eventually she leaves Sid's father to take up with a German lover but makes occasional returns to the marital bed.

Josie Long (plays Josie)

Josie Long is a writer for the series and also plays the Careers Advisor at Roundview College in series one and two. She approaches the job like a slightly deranged playschool teacher who is dealing with the offspring of hostile aliens. The scene where she tries to secure Chris a job as he appears before her in a variety of work uniforms is a brilliant piece of work in which she goes from bubbling enthusiasm to total despair in the face of his failure. Josie also appears at Chris's funeral, perhaps as an ironic comment on her failure to set him on the right path in life.

Sharing the same name as her character, Josie is from Orpington in Kent and began performing as a stand-up comedy at the tender age of 14.

She won the BBC New Comedy Awards at the age of 17 but gave up stand-up at 18 to read English Language

KATE MOLLOY

Josie Lawrence.

and Literature at Lady Margaret Hall, Oxford. She has contributed sketches to BBC Radio One's 2004 comedy show *The Milk Run* and won the Newcomer award at the Edinburg Fringe for her show 'Kindness and Exuberance'.

K is for...

Kathryn Prescott (plays Emily Fitch)

Kathryn Prescott is six minutes older than her twin sister Megan (who plays Katie) and she was born in Southgate, London. Although Kathryn had taken small TV roles in the past, true fame came when she accepted the role of Emily in the second series of *Skins*.

In 2008, Prescott and her sister Megan appeared in an episode of the television soap opera *Doctors* playing twin sisters Amy and Charlotte Wilcox. In March 2010, Prescott stated on her official website that she had landed a role in the TV pilot of a new thriller called *Goth*.

A fan of body art, Kathryn has at least 14 body piercings (although these are cleverly disguised onscreen) and her favourite bands include Röyksopp, The Cardigans and Metallica.

In response to a fan questioning her sexuality on her official website, Prescott answered that she would prefer to not label herself, stating that 'labels are for cans'. The question was prompted by the homosexuality of her character, Emily. Kathryn revealed that she received hundreds of letters from gay fans thanking her for helping them come to terms with their sexuality and says, 'I do not believe people are defined by their sexuality. It doesn't change who you are as a person.'

When shooting for a scene that shows Emily bathing with Naomi, it was so cold on set that Kathryn was taken to an onsite ambulance suffering with suspected hypothermia.

Katie Fitch (played by Megan Prescott)

In series two and three, Katie is the elder of the Fitch twins (born six minutes earlier) although in real life – for twin actresses Kathryn and Megan Prescott – it is the other way round.

Outspoken, aggressive and bullying, Katie doesn't need Emily around to be classed as double trouble. We meet her on the twins' first day of college and her selfish attitude towards her sister is revealed when she uses all the hot water and forces Emily to take a cold shower on her big day.

Stating that she has not been without a boyfriend since

OPPOSITE: KATHRYN PRESCOTT (EMILY FITCH) AND MEGAN PRESCOTT (KATIE FITCH) ARE TWIN SISTERS IN REAL LIFE.

the age of seven, Katie defines herself very much in relation to how attractive she is to men. She styles herself on a WAG, has a footballer boyfriend and wears far more revealing clothes than Emily does.

Arriving at college, and desperate for popularity, she immediately tries to befriend Effy. Realising that Naomi is also starting at Roundview, Katie, threatened by homosexuality, aggressively reveals that Naomi is a lesbian trying to seduce her straight sister.

Katie's homophobia is repellent to the rest of the gang, particularly Emily, who is gay and very attracted to Naomi. When Emily eventually tells Katie that she kissed Naomi and not the other way round, Katie cannot accept her sister's lesbianism and says, 'You're not gay, you're just stupid'. Try as she might to break them up, she does not succeed until eventually the two sisters come to blows, with Emily screaming that Katie has to let her be and not control her any longer.

We realise that, deep down, Katie is not actually homophobic but terrified of losing Emily and being alone. Lonely without Emily, and in need of attention, she strikes up a relationship with Freddie and sleeps with him even though she knows he is in love with Effy. Katie flaunts their relationship in front of Effy to make her jealous and while on a camping trip she pushes Effy to the ground and warns her to stay away from her man.

Effy – who is on a bad magic mushroom trip – bashes Katie over the head with a rock and leaves her unconscious in the woods. Being left alone all night in the woods and winding up in hospital is a pivotal moment in Katie's life. She realises that she needs to change and to grow up.

By series four, Katie is helping her mother run Let's Get Hitched, a wedding planning business. She is wearing more mature clothes and trying to be seen as a serious business-woman but life is about to deal her a series of horrible blows, shattering her confidence and aggressive facade.

Thinking she might be pregnant, Katie goes to the doctor. In a heartbreaking scene, the doctor tells her that her periods have stopped because she is going through an early menopause – she will never be able to have children.

The first person she wants to talk to is Emily, who has moved in with Naomi following her mother's refusal to accept their relationship. Unable to get hold of her she heads home to tell her mother but, when she gets there, her mum is in a desperate state after finding out the family is bankrupt. The next morning the bailiffs arrive to repossess their house and the Fitches have no option than to do a runner with as much stuff as they can. With nowhere to go they have no choice but to move into Naomi's house, much to Emily's chagrin. With her parents at each other's throats and Emily behaving like a crazy woman due to Naomi's affair, Katie is unable to tell anyone about the tragic news of her early menopause. She retreats to the bath and falls asleep. Without realising Katie is in there, Thomas comes in to use the loo and then gets locked in when the door jams.

Katie awakens and, in a moment of vulnerability, asks Thomas if he thinks she is bitch. Wisely, he answers that she is strong and that people need her around to tell them the truth. Needing to know she is still attractive now that she can't have kids Katie tells Thomas of her plight and kisses him. The kiss goes no further but he tells her that she a beautiful woman and any man would be lucky to have her.

Having bonded with Thomas, Katie resolves to make more effort and to stop being so aggressive with her friends. She pledges to help Thomas win back Pandora and helps Effy when she starts to suffer with her psychotic depression.

By the end of the series she is respected and cared for by the gang and feeling much happier. She has shown her caring side and looked after her family and friends. Most importantly, having finally accepted Emily's love affair with Naomi, she has won back the person she loves the most … her twin sister.

Kaya Scodelario (plays Effy Stonem)

With no prior acting experience Kaya Scodelario was cast as Effy Stonem in the first series of *Skins* at the age of 14. When she arrived at the auditions Kaya considered herself too young for the show and felt she was in the wrong place, but before she could leave she had been spotted by one of the producers and asked to read for the part. In the first series Effy had few speaking lines, but her enigmatic silences gave her an air of disquieting wisdom far beyond

OPPOSITE: BEAUTIFUL KAYA HAS MODELLED FOR *VOGUE*, *ELLE UK* AND *INSTYLE UK*.

her tender years, while the camera dwelled lovingly on her expressionless but beautifully-sculptured features.

Effy's role expanded as series one and two progressed until she became the central character in series three and four (she is the only character to remain) after all the original cast had been replaced with a new generation of characters. For her performance in *Skins* Kaya was nominated for *Best Actress* at the TV Quick Awards in 2009.

Kaya took her first film role in *Moon,* a sci-fi thriller which premiered at the 2009 Sundance Film Festival and earned critical acclaim. Last year she co-starred with her *Skins* onscreen brother Nicholas Hoult in the remake of *Clash of the Titans.* Kaya was also cast as Cathy in a new film adaptation of *Wuthering Heights* directed by Andrea Arnold.

As well as acting, Kaya has modelled for various magazines, including *Vogue, Dazed and Confused, Elle UK, Teen Vogue, Instyle UK,* and *i-D.*

Scodelario grew up fluent in Portuguese and English as her father is English and her mother from Brazil and she spends as much time in Brazil as she can. She has struggled with dyslexia throughout her life and has admitted that it has really dented her self-esteem at times.

As Effy, Kaya enjoyed a passionate on-screen love affair with Cook, played by Jack O'Donnell, and for a while they dated in real life. The relationship didn't last but they remain good friends.

Klariza Clayton (plays Karen McLair)

Karen is Freddie's older sister who is so desperate to become famous she appears on TV show called *Search for a Sexbomb* but loses when Cook – who has slept with her – fixes the votes. In series four Karen decides to do hairdressing at college and makes more appearances as she grows closer to Freddie. It is Karen who persuades Cook to look for Freddie when he goes missing; reminding him that Freddie looked out for him when he was on the run with Effy.

Klariza Clayton, from Croydon, is known for her television work that includes *Dani's House* and *House of Anubis*. Her career started with a role in the CBBC show *Young Dracula*. She starred opposite Michael Caine in the film *Harry Brown*, and also appeared as Lian in *EastEnders*. Klariza's mother is Filipino and her father is English.

L is for...

Laya Lewis (plays Liv Malone)

Yet another unknown before joining *Skins*, Laya, 18, is from Bristol where the show is set and filmed. The auditions took place in her school.

Laya loved filming in her home town and wasn't surprised when – despite the whole cast being new faces – passers-by immediately sussed that they were filming the new series.

Laya also has the enviable role (to the lads at least) of having the most sex scenes. As the devil may care, sexually confident Liv, Laya had to film the most explicit sex scene *Skins* has ever shown to date.

She admits the prospect terrified her and wished she'd had the confidence of her on-screen alter ego. 'She is really comfortable with herself, will eat a cheeseburger and get her baps outs,' Laya told the *Sun* newspaper. 'She gets loads of sex and doesn't care if people want to say bad things about her.

'In a way playing Liv empowered me. I didn't have a boyfriend when we started filming but by the end of it I had the confidence to chat up guys and I do have a lovely boyfriend now.'

Seeing your girlfriend onscreen having sex with lots of different boys could be hard for some people to handle but Laya says her boyfriend is really cool with it. She explained all the scenes to him in advance so he won't be shocked and has warned him not to take it seriously.

Lily Loveless (plays Naomi Campbell)

Having just turned 18, Lily was told not to bother going to the *Skins* auditions as she needed proof that she was 17 or younger. But having set her heart of being an actress, Lily had got herself an agent who put her up for a different set of auditions a month later. Luckily for Lily (and us) the producers took one look at her and knew she was perfect for Naomi.

'Apparently, when I am alone or just sitting there not talking to anyone I have a really screwed up look on my face,' laughs Lily. 'The casting director told me that when she saw that she thought, Wow, she's perfect for the part.'

Lily didn't tell anyone she was up for the part and recalls standing at a bus stop with some friends when she got the call to come to Bristol. And the rest is history.

THE CASTING DIRECTOR THOUGHT LILY WAS PERFECT FOR THE ROLE OF NAOMI AS SOON AS SHE SAW HER.

'It was the best feeling in the world,' she recalls. 'But as we were going to be a whole new cast taking over from a very popular one I was really scared that we would be hated.

Series three and four pushed even more boundaries than the original and came under fire as a bad influence on its viewers. Lily's character Naomi was part of one of the more controversial storylines known as 'Naomily' by fans, referring to her on-off lesbian relationship with Emily and their fears about coming out.

Defending the show, Lily says, 'I'd say that *Skins* isn't a show that tries to teach people about morals. Although some of the characters are doing certain things, their actions always have consequences. But it's not a show that's big on saying 'Do this and don't do that'. It's just a show that's meant to portray kids today, really. It's not trying to teach people lessons, and people shouldn't watch it like that.

'It's on after the watershed, so we can show a lot more than other shows. I think *Skins* is something a lot of people can relate to, because the actors are the same age as the characters they play, which is quite unusual. It might be a bit exaggerated, but that's what makes it all the more entertaining.'

As well as being a talented actress, Lily is a fabulous dancer and was a performer in Psychotic Dance Company, an award-winning dance group that specialises in street dance fused with other urban dance styles. In 2011, she also appeared in the Sky TV supernatural drama *Bedlam*.

Lisa Blackwell (plays Pandora Moon)

Having appeared briefly in the first two series as Effy's posh school friend Pandora, Lisa was thrilled when the producers of *Skins* wanted to expand Pandora as a main character in series three and four.

At just 16, with no professional acting experience, Lisa found the depiction of her character exploring a sex life very daunting. 'I was mortified during my first kissing scenes,' she recalls. 'I had only known Merveille, who plays my boyfriend Thomas, for a matter of days and I found it terribly embarrassing.'

Before appearing in *Skins,* Lisa, who was born and bred in Bristol, attended Stagecoach Theatre Arts School. In 2007 she began training with the National Youth Theatre.

In 2011, Lisa appeared in the West End Play *The Children's Hour,* alongside Hollywood heavyweights Keira Knightly and *Mad Men's* Elisabeth Moss.

It is Lisa's dream to appear in a lavish period drama and to play a villain because she feels she is so fresh faced and innocent looking, that playing a baddie would be the ultimate acting challenge.

Liv Malone (played by Laya Lewis)

Liv is like a breath of fresh air compared to her control freak best friend Mini. She loves to party, have wild sex and doesn't care what people think of her.

She is completely comfortable with her body and who

she is and doesn't give a monkey's about eating burgers and getting her boobs out.

Liv and Mini have been mates since primary school, but their relationship is tested very early in series five of *Skins* when Liv sleeps with Nick, Mini's boyfriend.

A sensitive side of Liv is revealed – she is riddled with guilt and vows to stay away from Nick. Even though Liv's patience is tested by Mini's bitching and arrogance, she still can't bear the thought of betraying her and hits the bottle and weed hard.

With no dad on the scene, Liv lives with her little sister and a mother who is always attending New Age seminars trying to find herself. In a surprising twist it is revealed that Liv has an older sister Bella, who is in prison. Her crime is not revealed but we see that Liv does not want to go the way of her sister and is trying to get her life straight.

Out shopping for booze, Liv encounters a handsome stranger and they agree to have one, wild day together with no names and no ties. After taking MDMA they hit some clubs and end up having sex in the open air.

The next day Liv discovers that her mystery man – Matty – is in fact Nick's black sheep brother.

Although ashamed of having had sex with both brothers, Liv cannot deny her feelings for Matty and they get together. What they don't know is that Nick is seething with jealousy and wants Liv to himself, which of course paves the way for more dramas ahead.

Adding to Liv's problems, Mini tells her she knows she slept with Nick and that she won't forgive her unless she drinks a bottle of vodka down in one to prove she is sorry. Full of remorse, Liv does as she says only to hear Mini tell her, 'I hope you die puking on your kidneys, you bitch.'

Luke Pasqualino (plays Freddie McLair)

Luke originally auditioned for the role of Tony in the first series but lost out to Nicholas Hoult. Undeterred, he came back for more and was thrilled to be cast as Freddie, the skateboarding hunk, who pines for Effy throughout most of series three and four.

Shooting the scenes that show Freddie deeply in love with Effy moved Luke to reflect on his own romantic life. He said at the time, 'Having played a character so consumed with love I think now that I have probably never actually been in love.

'I've had loads of girlfriends and liked them loads but I'm not sure it was real love.'

Before *Skins* – his first TV role – Luke had been a model, appeared in various plays and even worked in his sister's hairdressing salon. In a case of art imitating life, his *Skins* sister Karen trains to be a hairdresser and often uses Freddie as a model. The 20-year-old owes his gorgeous good looks to his Italian heritage – his father is Sicilian and his mother is Neapolitan.

Luke's character Freddie was dramatically killed off in series four, an event which came as a shock to the cast and even more so to the fans. Luke recalled in an interview with Digital Spy:

THE VERY
SEXY LUKE
PASQUALINO.

'There were loads of complaints apparently, which is nice because it shows I was a popular character. I found out about it three weeks before we filmed it. My producer took me out for a meal and he cut to the chase. At first I thought he was having me on and then I found out he wasn't, obviously!

'Whether I liked it or not, it was going to happen so I thought, make the most of it. I enjoyed filming it and working with Hugo Speer [who plays Dr Foster, the man who murdered Freddie] so it was good.'

Since leaving *Skins*, Luke has filmed *The Apparition*, a Warner Bros supernatural thriller, alongside Ashley Greene star of *Twilight*.

M is for...

Mackenzie Crook (plays Johnny White)

Popular actor and comedian Mackenzie Crook is best known for playing Ragetti in the *Pirates of the Caribbean* films and Gareth Keenan in *The Office*. Crook was born in Maidstone, England, at the age of 15 he joined the Orchard Youth Theatre in Dartford. He tried stand up comedy in the guise of Charlie Cheese, 'the cheeky chirpy chappy from Chorley'.

Along with Ali G creator Sasha Baron Cohen, Crook was spotted by Bob Mortimer at the 1998 Edinburgh Festival, and the pair were offered their first major television roles as comedy sketch contributors on Channel 4's *The Eleven O'clock Show*.

In 2001, Crook auditioned for and won a role in *The*

Office, going on to receive two BAFTA nominations for his performance.

Crook played Ragetti, a pirate with a false eye, in *Pirates of the Caribbean: The Curse of the Black Pearl* (2003), *Pirates of the Caribbean: Dead Man's Chest* (2006) and in *Pirates of the Caribbean: At Worlds End* (2007). He also appeared as Lancelot Gobbo in the 2004 film *The Merchant of Venice*. Other films he has appeared in include *The Gathering*, *The Brothers Grimm* and the BBC adaptation of Charles Dickens' *Little Dorrit*.

He starred with Kristin Scott Thomas in director Ian Rickson's production of *The Seagull*, for which he earned a nomination from the Evening Standard Theatre Awards. Starting at the Royal Court Theatre in London in February 2007, the show transferred to Broadway in September 2008. In December 2008 he finished the Broadway run of *The Seagull* at the Walter Kerr Theatre.

From July 15, Mackenzie appeared at the Royal Court Theatre in Jez Butterworth's *Jerusalem*. He and the play received rave reviews.

Crook and his wife Lindsay have a son and a daughter, and live in Peter Sellers' former house in London's Muswell Hill.

Madison 'Mad' Twatter (played by Stephen Walters)

Twatter first appeared in the first episode of series one. Tony dispatches Sid to buy an ounce of marijuana from of him so they can sell the excess at a party. Sid finds Twatter in the slightly surreal surroundings of a chintzily decorated suburban brothel inhabited by scantily clad working girls. Mad Twatter is clearly insane, and his crazy appearance is enhanced by a huge black handlebar moustache and flaring eyes. He terrifies Sid into accepting three ounces of spliff on credit at a vast interest rate, to be paid in the future. Later that evening, a car Sid is travelling in skids off the road into a canal, and fully submerged, he loses his spliff. Mad Twatter eventually manages to catch up with Sid when he is out with his friend Jal and he destroys her valuable clarinet. Jal's brothers attempt to protect her but Twatter beats them up. However, retribution finally comes. Jal's father and his bodyguards capture Twatter and we last see him howling in rage as he is being driven away to what we imagine is a final resting place. Stephen Martin Walters, who plays Mad Twatter, is a British actor who has taken film roles in *Mean Machine*, *The 51st State*, *Batman Begins*, *Layer Cake*, *Revolver*, and *Hannibal Rising*. He also plays a barman in *East is East*. He has starred in numerous television productions.

Magic Mushrooms

In series three the gang decided to go on a camping trip in some local woods and take along what they call some 'special fungi' to get in the party spirit. This leads to trouble: Effy hits Katie over the head with a rock after Katie discovers her boyfriend and Effy having sex.

According to FRANK (www.talktofrank.com), the government run drug education service; magic mushrooms produce similar hallucinogenic effects to LSD. There are two main types of mushroom and they're quite different. The most common form is a species called 'liberty cap', the other more potent variety is known as 'fly agaric'. The biggest danger with taking any magic mushrooms is making sure you've picked the right mushroom – there are hundreds of varieties and some of them are highly poisonous. FRANK says that both types of mushrooms can make you feel sick, tired and disoriented.

Magic mushrooms can complicate any mental health issues you may have. FRANK says that the effects kick in from 30 minutes to two hours after consumption, and the full effects can last for ten hours with after effects of anything up to six hours. Both types of mushrooms can make you feel relaxed, confident, and cheerful. Reality may become distorted, and the senses scrambled, so you may think you can see sounds and feel colours. Time and space may also become distorted. Some say they experience greater emotions and sensitivities and become more creative or enlightened. 'Bad trips' are seriously frightening and unsettling, and you can't tell whether you're going to have a bad trip or a good trip. Also you can get flashbacks for some time afterwards. Slang terms for drugs vary around the country – they are known as magic mushrooms, liberty caps, Liberties, Amani, mushies, shrooms, magics, or agaric. Magic mushrooms are classified as Class A drugs. Those in possession can be sentenced to seven years in jail and an unlimited fine.

Maureen Lipman (plays Aunt Elizabeth)

Playing spliff-head Aunt Elizabeth was a lot of fun for one of our best known and much loved actresses. With a huge body of work behind her, Lipman is one of the UK's most prolific actresses and it was a real coup for the production when she agreed to guest star.

London born Maureen trained at the London Academy of Music and Dramatic Art and has worked extensively in the theatre. She was a member of Laurence Olivier's original Royal National Theatre Company at the Old Vic. Maureen made an early film appearance in *Up the Junction* and starred in the 1979 television comedy *Agony*. She is well-known for playing Joyce Grenfell in the biographical show *Re: Joyce!*, which she co-wrote. She has worked in the theatre, films, radio and television for over thirty years. Recently, she starred in the National Theatre's production of *Oklahoma!*

In 2002, she appeared as a guest star in *Coronation Street*, and in Roman Polanski's award-winning film *The Pianist*. A prolific writer, she wrote a monthly column for *Good Housekeeping* magazine for more than ten years. This led to several books. More recently, she wrote a weekly column in *The Guardian*.

After her husband Jack Rosenthal's death in 2004, Lipman finished his autobiography *By Jack*. She has

MAUREEN LIPMAN.

two children, writers Amy Rosenthal and Adam Rosenthal. Lipman is a Labour Party supporter and is on the editorial advisory board of *Jewish Renaissance* magazine. Lipman also supports the work of the Burma Campaign UK.

She was awarded the *Laurence Olivier Theatre Award* for Best Comedy Performance in 1985 (1984 season) for *See How They Run*. She was awarded an honorary doctorate from the University of Hull in 1994, and was awarded the CBE in 1999.

As a tireless and much-loved performer, Lipman's recent appearance in *Skins* as Pandora's Aunt Elizabeth has made her known to a whole new generation of fans.

Maxxie Oliver (played by Mitch Hewer)

Maxxie, a brilliant dancer, is a popular and well-adjusted character who is proud of being gay. He can be persuasive, convincing Anwar and Chris to join him on a 'Big Gay Night Out', which turns out to be something of a disaster, causing them to change plans and go to posh Abigail's party. On a school trip to Russia, Maxxie and Anwar's friendship is challenged because Anwar's faith condemns homosexuality. Maxxie says Anwar – who is a Muslim – is homophobic and hypocritical because although Anwar disapproves of gay people, he is prepared to have pre-marital sex, take drugs and drink alcohol even though they are forbidden by his religion. Eventually, Maxxie tries again to get Anwar to accept him being gay, but Anwar refuses. Maxxie walks away with tears in his eyes.

Later, Tony tries to give oral sex to Maxxie, which he refuses. He tells Tony that he isn't very good at it. Tony's girlfriend, Michelle witnesses the whole scene. Tony continues to flirt with Maxxie, who apologises to Michelle for the incident with Tony in Russia. He is devastated when she accuses him of being a 'dirty little slut who fucks around with other people's boyfriends'.

Later, guilty over Tony and Michelle's recent breakup, Maxxie claims that it was his fault, saying 'I lost my head and then he gave me head', despite the fact that everything that happened had been at Tony's instigation. Eventually, Maxxie calls Anwar to wish him a happy birthday, but he refuses to attend the party unless Anwar tells his parents that Maxxie is gay. Anwar, keen to see Maxxie again, finds him waiting outside and refusing to go in. Anwar's father eventually arrives and spots Maxxie. The two talk until Anwar interrupts to tell his father that Maxxie is gay. Mr Kharral seemingly ignores what Anwar has said until Maxxie says it himself. In a moving scene, Mr Kharral explains that there are a lot of things in the world he doesn't understand, particularly homosexuality, but his faith in Allah means he believes God one day will reveal to him all he does not understand. Until then, he says, he will treat Maxxie no differently. Maxxie and Anwar's friendship is restored.

OPPOSITE: MAXXIE WAS A POPULAR CHARACTER PORTRAYED PERFECTLY BY ACTOR MICTH HEWER.

After Tony's car accident and his subsequent brain trauma, Maxxie, Jal and Chris are the only friends who stay close to him. Maxxie tries to get his dad, Walter, to agree to let him drop his A Levels and audition for musicals in London. But his dad refuses, wanting him to join him in his business when he gets his A Levels. Maxxie comes from a decent home with loving parents, but he still receives homophobic abuse from the roughs on the council estate where he lives. It later turns out that one of the chavs who persecute him is also gay. Eventually, when Walter has had time to reflect on his relationship with his son, they agree that Maxxie will continue his A Levels even if he does not eventually join his father as a builder. Sketch, another student at Roundview College who lives in a flat opposite Maxxie's (where she cares for her ailing mother), begins to stalk Maxxie. She takes pictures of him and pins them up on the wall of her bedroom; she also leaves Maxxie gifts in his locker at college. Knowing he is gay, she tries to make herself appear masculine by flattening her chest. Sketch is part of the drama group. At a party thrown by Mr Gelcart, the drama teacher, Maxxie — unaware that Sketch is obsessed with him attempts to set her up with Anwar, who is desperate for a girlfriend. On the morning after the party, Maxxie realises that Sketch is pathologically obsessed when he discovers she broke into his flat and has slept under his bed. Maxxie retaliates by humiliating Sketch in front of the audience when she takes Michelle's place in the school musical by refusing to kiss her in the love scene. Eventually, Sketch begins a relationship with Anwar in order to be nearer to Maxxie. Finally, Maxxie meets someone to love, a youth called James. Maxxie proudly introduces James to everyone at college. In the last episode, Maxxie and James move to London together, and Maxxie persuades Anwar to go with them. He does so, and abandons Sketch at the bus stop.

Megan Prescott (Katie Fitch)

London-born Megan Prescott claims that her absolute dream role would be as someone's long lost relative in *Desperate Housewives*. She is best known for her role as Katie Fitch in *Skins*. Megan is six minutes younger than her twin sister Kathryn Prescott, who is also an actor. Megan studied television production and directing at university. Before they began acting professionally, Megan and her sister attended drama classes where they met their future co-star Lily Loveless. In a MySpace Live Webchat, Prescott revealed that she plays the drums. Her music tastes include Weezer, Kim Carnes, and Cyndi Lauper. Along with sister Kathryn, Megan made her acting debut in 2008 in an episode of the BBC soap opera *Doctors*, but it wasn't until the following year – when she appeared as Katie Fitch in the third series of *Skins* – that she considered she'd made a breakthrough in acting.

Since the format is limited to only two series for each 'generation', Prescott was worried about her future as an actress when her series of *Skins* series was finished. But she has come to realise that insecurity is one of the

MEGAN WITH HER SISTER AND
CO-STARS ON THE RED CARPET!

standard worries of the profession. She is a big fan of the American television show *Desperate Housewives* and has ambitions to work on the show. On her sister's official blog Kathryn revealed that she and her sister may take a gap year to volunteer with an animal sanctuary either in Malaysia or Florida.

Merveille Lukeba (plays Thomas Tomone)

Playing Thomas very nearly didn't happen for Merveille, known as Merv to his friends. The original character was meant to be Polish and the writers only decided to change it a few days before shooting.

Skins director Simon Massey says it presented a huge challenge to find the right actor for the role. 'We needed someone who was from the Congo, could speak French and be able to carry a whole episode. And we needed him at very short notice. Merv was fantastic. Thank God we found him.'

Born in 1990 in Kinshasa, Democratic Republic of the Congo, Merv's family then moved to Woolwich, South London, where Merv was raised. His on-screen debut came in 2006 as Sierra Leonian child soldier Moses in film *Ezra*, which was shown at the Sundance Film Festival.

Skins was something of a shock to Merv. 'Because they changed their minds about my character at very short notice, I hadn't got to know anyone before I had to shoot my parts. On my second day of filming I had to shoot a shower scene and there I was, in front of 80 people I didn't know, completely butt naked. '

MERVILLE LUKEBA'S CHARACTER THOMAS WAS ORIGINALLY MEANT TO BE POLISH BUT LUCKY FOR MERV THE DIRECTORS CHANGED THEIR MIND AND BEGAN LOOKING FOR A NEW THOMAS!

But even more of a challenge for Merv was convincingly depicting Thomas's passion for doughnuts. 'They are Thomas's favourite food and he thinks nothing of eating a whole box,' says Merv. 'I will never forget that first day filming when I had to keep eating and eating them. After a few takes I threw up. I couldn't face another doughnut for about six months.'

Michelle Richardson (played by April Pearson)

When we first meet Michelle, she appears to be only interested in catering to her boyfriend Tony Stonem's whims and 'looking shaggable', which she views as her first duty and compares it with her best friend Jal's passion for the clarinet. Unsure of herself as a person, Michelle cannot see any other good qualities in herself other than looking gorgeous so she puts all her efforts into grooming herself.

Michelle is proud and sensitive about her looks and on her fictional *Skins* website page in the 'About me' section, she insists that her pictures have not been Photoshopped, and she is 'this gorgeous in real life'.

Michelle becomes angry when Tony claims that her breasts are uneven, and refers to her nipples as 'nips'. Knowing that Tony's friend, Sid, is in love with her, she sometimes wonders if he would be a better boyfriend than Tony.

In spite of her apparent lack of disinterest in schoolwork, she is multi-lingual, speaking French, Italian and Spanish.

Jamie Brittain's original concept for the show included Michelle, but at first he was going to call her Annie. When Brittain was a teenager, he began an unfinished novel that included the characters of Sid, Tony and Michelle, and he revived them when he began the television series.

In the first episode, Michelle demonstrates how she is manipulated by Tony, when, at his suggestion, she persuades one of her best friends, Cassie, to take Sid's virginity, a plot that fails. Later she becomes concerned by Tony's attraction to posh girl Abigail and reflects that Tony will never love her in the way Sid does.

As further proof of Tony's manipulative treatment of Michelle, he openly kisses Abigail at a concert and later allows Michelle to see him fondling her breasts. Furious, Michelle breaks up with him. After a street encounter with a gang of chavvy girls who assault her, Michelle is distraught and confronts Sid, whom she accuses of being part of her humiliation by Tony. Then Tony urges Sid to try and seduce Michelle while she is on the rebound. It looks as if Michelle will get together with Sid, but Tony reappears and makes Sid watch as he takes Michelle back, once again reaffirming his power over them both.

On a school trip in Russia, Michelle and Jal go out to a bar and get drunk with a group of Russian soldiers. Back in the room she is sharing with Tony, he thinks she has passed out, but she witnesses Tony's failed attempt to seduce Maxxie. On the flight home Michelle tries to get Tony to explain his actions but she fails.

Michelle finally breaks up with Tony. Jal asks if Tony

cheated again, and Michelle is deeply hurt when she discovers Jal has always known about Tony's infidelities, including with Abigail. Maxxie also asks her not to tell anybody what had happened in Russia.

Michelle becomes depressed and is discovered drinking in the school supply room by Angie, the psychology teacher. Despite her unhappiness, she remains determined not to see Tony again, and rebuffs his efforts to win her back. At home she's angered by Malcolm, her mother's latest husband. She thinks he is unpleasant, unfeeling and only using her mother for his own ends.

Michelle meets Abigail's brother, Josh, and is attracted to him. Once again, Tony tries to get back with her, but Michelle demands he 'prove' that he really loves her. Unconvinced by Tony, she turns to Sid, who has been in love with her for years, only to realise that he has come to love her as just a friend. Michelle takes Sid to see Cassie, who Sid now loves. She is back in rehab after a suicide attempt. At the clinic, she meets Josh, who is a nurse. He asks her out on a date.

Michelle enjoys Josh's company as, unlike the coldly detached Tony, he treats her as an equal. She discovers that Josh is prescribed medication by his mother, a psychiatrist at the rehab clinic, but this does not affect their relationship. Tony has been spying on her, and manages to sabotage their relationship when he steals Josh's mobile and downloads pornographic pictures he has taken of Abigail. He sends them to Michelle as if they have come from Josh's telephone. Michelle is repelled by the pictures, and disgusted with Josh, who she thinks has sent the porn pictures of his sister to her because of a perverted mental condition. Later, Tony makes another attempt to fix things with Michelle, but she still rejects him.

In the finale of series one, Michelle meets Tony's sister Effy, who was just recently been involved in a chilling incident where she has been kidnapped and drugged by Josh in order to humiliate Tony for the business of Abigail's telephone pictures. Michelle asks her why Tony hurt her, but Effy genuinely doesn't know. Later, Michelle attends Anwar's birthday party. Tony is also going to attend, accompanied by Effy. Before either go inside, Effy calls Tony a 'wanker' for hurting Michelle. Spurred by the confrontation with his sister, Tony calls Michelle on his mobile to say how much he loves her. Michelle cries while he is talking and, as Tony crosses the street while on the phone, he is hit by a bus. At the end of the episode, Michelle is seen calling an ambulance.

In the second series, we learn that Michelle has had no contact with Tony during the six months following his accident. Instead, she has been seeing other men, and presumably having sex with them. It's clear that she is unhappy and confused by the situation with Tony, and aware of how wrong her action has been. As well as her difficulties with Tony, her relationship with Sid is awkward – he has seen her flirting at a club with other men and snogging them. When she realises that Sid has seen her she runs out of the club ashamed. Outside, Michelle confesses to Sid that she has only visited Tony once since the accident.

School resumes and Michelle is now in her final year. Michelle signs up for the school play *Osama! The Musical*. As she has a talent for singing, she is cast in the lead role alongside Maxxie. During a rehearsal, Maxxie is called on to kiss Michelle. A jealous Sketch, Maxxie's stalker, almost kills Michelle by dropping a heavy stage light that only just misses her.

At a costume fund raising party for the drama department, Michelle comes as Princess Leia from *Star Wars*. Abigail, also dressed as Leia, insults her. To compound the insult she has come with Tony, who is dressed as Luke Skywalker. Michelle is wounded that Tony has dressed to compliment Abigail. Yet Tony himself – still confused by his brain injuries – is unclear why he is wearing his costume. He still doesn't understand his relationship with Abigail. We learn from a private conversation between Michelle and Tony that Abigail has been convincing Tony she is his girlfriend. Michelle makes a failed attempt to seduce Tony, and is deeply wounded that Tony actually doesn't remember what they were to each other. Finally, Michelle realises that Tony isn't the person he was before the accident.

Sketch falsely accuses the odious drama teacher Bruce of assaulting her, and Michelle befriends Sketch by inviting her to sit with her during lunch. Michelle only discovers Sketch's true colours when Sketch dopes her with pills that make her sick and cause her to drop out of the school play moments before the curtain goes up.

Later, Michelle questions Tony again on how much he

remembers of their previous relationship. He tells her hardly anything. She tries to seduce him but because of his brain damage, he cannot get an erection. Frustrated, Michelle slaps him, blaming Tony for the accident and his present condition. She apologises, but says she cannot wait for him, and the two finally end their relationship. Before leaving, Tony gives her an early birthday gift, and Michelle invites him on her planned birthday camping trip, but he declines.

We learn that Michelle's mother has ended her relationship with Malcolm and married one of her clients, a dreadful poseur called Ted. They have moved into Ted's hi-tech home, which Michelle hates. To compound matters, Ted has a spoiled daughter, Scarlett, who decides to move in as well and also attend Roundview College. At school, Scarlett proves to be a hit with Michelle's friends. She invites herself on Michelle's camping trip, offering the use of her car. On the trip Michelle feels alone and is constantly irritated by the presence of Scarlett. Later that night, she catches Scarlett trying to seduce Sid and decides to confront her. But it doesn't work out as expected. Michelle discovers that Scarlett is nicer than she had thought. Michelle goes after Sid, who is feeling very low.

In a moving scene, Sid confesses his grief over his recently deceased father, and they make love for the first time on the beach. But they're not yet ready to tell their friends, so decide to keep their relationship secret. When the trip is over, the pair return to Sid's home, where their friend Cassie is waiting and discovers they are in a sexual relationship.

Cassie tells the gang of Michelle and Sid's new relationship, and everyone is astonished. Tony pretends not to care, but Jal – Michelle's best friend – is angry that he wasn't told. Later, during one night at a club, Tony confronts Michelle and Sid, who are having sex in the toilet. Tony tells Michelle that she should be with him, and that Sid should really still be with Cassie. Sid admits that he isn't in love with Michelle anymore, and Michelle is shocked by Sid's change of heart and Tony's determination to win her back.

Tony continues trying to win Michelle, but she ignores his calls and text messages. She still claims she wants nothing to do with him, and even returns a watch he gave her for her birthday (the watch also happens to be broken). But Effy gets the watch fixed and engraved with the word 'forever' and sends it back to Michelle, who is finally moved enough to take Tony's phone call. She answers the phone, saying, 'I love you, too' before hanging it up again.

Later, we learn that Michelle and Tony are trying to take their relationship 'slow' and not 'make a thing of it'. Michelle continues to worry – exams are upon them, and Jal needs Michelle as she is mourning the death of Chris. Michelle and Tony seem happy together. Tony brings her flowers, and carries her books to class.

But when Michelle receives her A level results: 2 As and 1 B, she plans to go to York University, while Tony plans to go to Cardiff. Finally, Michelle and Tony are unsure whether they're going to continue their relationship or break up for good.

Mike Bailey (plays Sid Jenkins)

Mike Bailey is an actor and singer from Bristol best known for playing the role of Sid Jenkins in the first two series of *Skins*. In the role, he was called on to sing 'Wild World' by Cat Stevens. Bailey has also appeared in the Channel 4 drama *1066: The Battle for Middle Earth,* which was broadcast in 2009. On the character he plays, Bailey told Digital Spy:

He gets bullied a lot. He doesn't realise it, especially from Tony. It's not the bullying you see every day – not the physical, the mental, but Sid sticks with it.' He adds, 'I'm at college at the moment doing performing arts and the only things I've done before were plays and stuff at college. I haven't even been an extra on Casualty, which it seems that everyone in Bristol had! So, this is the first big thing for me, and it's such a good experience to go from doing absolutely nothing to being a lead character on TV. I'm so proud of myself for getting it, I'm so glad I got it. Not many people can say they had the same possibilities and experience as me. I'm well chuffed with myself.

KATE MOLLOY

ACTOR MIKE BAILEY.

In response to a question about the sex scenes he said:

> When you're filming it, you don't really think about it. The full naked shots, which all of the male members of the cast had to do at some point, were really different to what you expect it to be – everyone's so professional when you're there. The cast and the crew all sympathise and help you realise it's not the easiest thing to do. When I'm under the covers doing what needs to be done, everyone was having a laugh with that, because it's something everyone can have a laugh with, admit they did it, everyone's talked about it. It's not that bad doing it, but when I have to sit down with my family and watch doing it – well, that's a whole different story.

Minerva 'Mini' McGuiness (played by Freya Mavor)

Mini appears to have it all. Luscious long blonde hair, endless legs, an enviable figure and the heart of Nick, the college sporting hero. While everyone at college sees Mini as perfect, they don't know she is hiding a secret. Lurking underneath all that glamour is a person riddled with insecurities and low self-esteem. Mini is controlling, bitchy and shallow, caring more what people wear than what kind of a person they are, and she wants to hang on to her college Queen Bee status at all costs.

Giving the impression that she is fantastic in bed and

very sexually experienced, Mini is in fact a virgin and terrified of making love with boyfriend Nick. He thinks she is just playing hard to get and constantly pressures her into having sex. Mini, though, hates her body and adheres to a ridiculously rigid diet regime, weighing every sultana and nut she puts in her breakfast cereal. The thought of taking her clothes off in front of Nick fills her with horror – when she knows that time is running out, she has to get drunk before going to bed with him.

Pretending that she is experienced, Mini attempts to perform oral sex but all the booze and her nerves get the better of her and she throws up all over Nick, who is understandably not best pleased.

Nick, confused as to why Mini doesn't seem to want his body, seeks comfort in her best friend Liv, and they begin an affair. Mini is heartbroken but so needy that, knowing he doesn't love her and is sleeping with her best friend, she carries on seeing Nick. To Mini, appearances are everything and there is no way she is going to be laughed at by the students of Roundview and lose her status as Queen Bee.

Mitch Hewer (plays Maxxie Oliver)

Mitchell Hewer is best known for his role of Maxxie Oliver. He has also starred as Danny Miller in *Britannia High*. At the end of the second series of *Skins*, his character (like the rest of the main cast) was written out of the show to make way for another generation. Mitch trained at SWADA (South West Academy of Dramatic Arts) in Bristol and appeared on the cover of gay lifestyle magazine *Attitude* in the issue featuring 'Gays on TV'. It included stars from *Coronation Street, Shameless, Hollyoaks* and *Skins*. He was also featured nude in *Cosmopolitan* in aid of testicular cancer research.

Hewer has done a great deal of photographic modelling. He also appeared with host Holly Willoughby as a guest panellist in the popular ITV2 show *Xtra Factor*. He has made an appearance on the BBC comedy show *Never Mind the Buzzcocks* alongside team captain Davina McCall and singer Alesha Dixon. He has filled slots on ITV's *This Morning* as well as *Richard and Judy's New Position*.

In December 2009, Hewer appeared in the musical *Never Forget*. He played stripper Dirty Harry alongside Michelle Collins.

Morwenna Banks (plays Anthea Stonem)

Playing unlucky-in-love mum of Tony and Effy is Morwenna Banks, a comedy actress, writer and producer. In the third series of *Skins*, her character Anthea has an affair with her husband's boss Steve (played by her real-life partner David Baddiel).

Morwenna came to prominence in the Channel 4 series *Absolutely*. Her television work includes roles in the series *Sabrina, the Teenage Witch*, and the BBC comedy series *Catterick* with Vic Reeves and Bob Mortimer. She spoke the part of Clare Feeble, in *Stressed Eric*, Mummy Pig in the children's animated series *Peppa Pig,* as well as the voices of the witches in *Meg and Mog*, a 2003 animated children's series for CITV.

As an impressionist Morwenna made a series of web videos for the BBC comedy *Celebrities STFU*, where she cleverly impersonated celebrities Noel Gallagher, Pixie Lott, Lady Gaga, Jools Holland, Susan Boyle, and Duffy. Banks also appears with Angus Deayton and Tony Hawks in the film *Playing the Moldovans at Tennis*.

N is for...

Naomi Campbell (played by Lily Loveless)

Naomi works hard at her college work and is a principled political activist. She is less frivolous than the rest of the gang but she still knows how to party.

At the beginning of series three, we see Naomi tell her friends that she is definitely into guys. But the truth is that, deep down, she is struggling with her feelings for Emily and their burgeoning relationship. This struggle forms most of Naomi's plotlines in the series. She faces a lot of homophobia from Emily's twin sister Katie, but handles it with dignity and grace.

Naomi's hippy mother Gina, played by Olivia Colman, believes in free love and communal living. This annoys Naomi massively, and in one episode she wakes up to find an unknown male hippy sleeping in her bed.

Trying to distract herself from Emily, Naomi considers running for college President, but Emily becomes involved in her campaign. At first distant, Naomi allows Emily to help her try to stop students from voting for Cook. She also begins to rely on the advice of her politics teacher Kieran. Arriving home, Naomi finds Emily in her bedroom with plans for the campaign and, frightened of what might happen between them, is standoffish. Emily starts to leave but then boldly returns to tell Naomi that she is not obsessed with pursuing a sexual relationship. Naomi suggests she stay the night but just as friends.

Naomi leaves Emily sleeping in the morning and heads to college. She is shocked to see how much popularity Cook's campaign is gaining. She tries to speak seriously to the students but is humiliated by Cook, who has anarchist ideas and just wants to party. Emily stands up for Naomi, but she flees to teacher Kieran for comfort. She is horrified when Kieran tries to kiss her – she had believed he was interested in her as a person and a student not a sexual being. Naomi cries herself to sleep.

The next day, Emily suggests a trip to a lake – Naomi's favourite beauty spot – to cheer her up. They cycle there, laughing and enjoying themselves, and after a swim they proceed to make love. Naomi wants to flee again and, devastated, Emily cries that she cannot leave her hanging for a second time. Confused, Naomi arrives home, only to walk in on her mother in bed with Kieran.

When she arrives at college, she discovers that the teachers have rigged the vote in her favour to prevent

Cook from succeeding. Although she really wants to win, her principles will not allow her to cheat. She exposes the scam (which earns her Cook's respect), and Cook incites the students into a victory riot. In the ensuing chaos, Cook attempts to have sex with Naomi, but after kissing him she says 'it's just not right' and goes in search of Emily.

Emily refuses to open her front door as she has been crying so much and, in a very tender scene, the two girls hold hands through the cat flap.

Series four begins with Naomi and Emily very much a couple. They have enjoyed a wonderful summer of love. Although Emily wants them to travel to Mexico when college finishes, Naomi has secretly been attending university open days and wants to continue her education. With continuing problems at home – Emily's mother is unable to accept their lesbian relationship – Emily moves in with Naomi while her mother is on an extended break in France.

After witnessing the suicide of Sophia, a young girl high on MDMA at a nightclub, Emily becomes suspicious of Naomi's strange behaviour when they are questioned by police. Eventually Naomi admits that she sold the MDMA to the dead girl to get money to buy Emily a present. Naomi denies that she knew the girl, but Emily turns detective and discovers that Naomi met Sophia while on a secret visit to a London university and had a one-day love affair. Naomi's subsequent rejection of her caused Sophia to take her life.

Naomi is devastated at having hurt Emily but cannot get

her to forgive her. Their relationship becomes horribly strained and they hit breaking point. Emily completely loses the plot when Emily's family hit the buffers and have to move in with the two girls. She lashes out at her mother, her twin and most of all Naomi for hurting her so much, telling her she has ruined everything.

When Emily strikes up a friendship with Mandy, a secret lesbian, Naomi is not worried as she believes Mandy likes guys. She even puts them to bed together one night when they are trashed and sleeps on the sofa. The next morning, unable to break down Emily's anger, Naomi hits the weed and booze. As Naomi dances provocatively Mandy joins in and kisses her, telling her if she doesn't treat Emily right, she will. This gives Naomi food for thought and she contemplates how she can win Emily's trust again.

In the final episode, the gang are partying in Freddie's shed and a tearful Naomi arrives to speak to Emily. At first Emily is reluctant but in a beautiful speech Naomi describes how she truly feels. Heartbreakingly, she says to Emily in front of the whole crowd:

'I've loved you from the first time I saw you. I think I was 12. It took me three years to pluck up the courage to speak to you, and I was so scared of the way I felt, you know, loving a girl, that I learned how to become a sarcastic bitch just to make it feel normal. I screwed guys to make it go away, but it didn't work. When we got together, it scared the shit out of me, because...

you were the one person who could ruin my life. I pushed you away and made you think things were your fault, but really I was just terrified of pain. I screwed that girl Sophia to kind of spite you for having a hold on me, and I'm a total fucking coward because… I got… these tickets to Goa for us three months ago. But I… I couldn't stand… I didn't want to be a slave to the way I feel about you. Can you understand? You were trying to punish me back, and it's horrible. It's so horrible because… Really, I'd die for you. I love you. I love you so much it's killing me.'

Known to fans as 'Naomily', Naomi and Emily's storylines were highly regarded within the lesbian community. Sarah Warn, Editor-in-Chief of lesbian-based website AfterEllen.com, wrote that the 'Naomily' was one of the best-developed and most honest depictions of a lesbian teenage relationship that she'd ever seen on TV.

Lily Loveless, who plays Naomi, was very proud to be part of such an intrinsic and significant plotline. 'I received lots of letters from as far away as Peru and Australia and some fans even sent presents,' she said during an interview with E4 youth show T4.

'One thing that really sticks in my mind though is I was in a club once, and these two girls came up to me, and they were friends, and they said "Watching your story made us come out to each other, and now we're dating." It was amazing. I was so happy for them.'

Neil Morrissey (plays Marcus Ainsworth, Cassie's Dad)

Playing Cassie's amateur artist Dad (who has a passion for painting her mum in the nude) is Neil Morrissey. Best known for his role as Tony in *Men Behaving Badly* and deputy head Eddie Lawson in *Waterloo Road*, Neil is also much loved by millions of children the world over as the voice of Bob the Builder.

His early life was a tough one. Born in Stafford, Neil and his brothers were placed under a care order and legally separated from their parents. They spent their childhood in separate foster homes, and Neil spent most of his time at the Penkhull Children's Home.

He studied his A Levels at the City of Stoke-on-Trent Sixth Form College. During this time he was a member of the Stoke Repertory Theatre, Stoke Schools Theatre, and Stoke Original Theatre, and performed at the Edinburgh Fringe. He subsequently gained an unconditional scholarship allowing him to study at the Guildhall School of Music and Drama. On leaving Guildhall, Morrissey paid his student debts with money earned in film roles.

His first part was in 1984 as Able Seaman Matthew Quintal in *The Bounty* alongside Mel Gibson, Anthony Hopkins and Laurence Olivier. Morrissey found fame as biker Rocky in the ITV drama series *Boon*. In 1990, he took the lead role of *Noddy* in the spoof horror film *I Bought a Vampire Motorcycle*, which involved many of the cast from *Boon*. His role as Tony in *Men Behaving Badly* was created to replace the character of Dermot after Harry

NEIL MORRISSEY IS PROBABLY BEST KNOWN AS HIS CHARACTER TONY IN *MEN BEHAVING BADLY*.

Enfield left the show. The series made Morrissey a star. He starred in the John Godber film about rugby league called *Up n Under*. On the West End stage his work includes *Speed*, *Robin Hood*, *The Daughter-In-Law* and *A Passionate Woman*. Morrissey also played alongside Julie Walters, Celia Imrie, Duncan Preston and Josie Lawrence in Victoria Wood's musical adaptation of *Acorn Antiques The Musical*, and went on to take the role of Nathan Detroit in the London revival of *Guys and Dolls*. In *Skins*, he appeared as Cassie's father. In 2007 he appeared in the BBC's *Waterloo Road* as the new deputy head teacher, Eddie. A shrewd businessman, Morrissey has invested in various projects, including production companies and his own television advertising and production company, Cactus Media Group. He has also invested in hotels and pubs. In 2006 he was awarded an honorary degree from Staffordshire University.

Nick Levan (played by Sean Teale)

Hot bod, hot girlfriend and the hottest player on the rugby field, Nick is the college jock with the world at his feet.

Hero-worshipped by his teammates and fancied by all the girls, Nick is a winner in every sense – until he sleeps with Liv, his girlfriend's best friend. After this, Nick's life begins to unravel.

With the biggest game of his life looming, Nick is meant to be training hard and sticking to a healthy lifestyle. But his obsession with Liv and constant pressure from his overbearing and competitive father sends Nick into meltdown. We soon learn that Nick's home life consists of no Mum and a Dad who cannot bare failure of any kind. He bullies Nick to do well constantly and has thrown Nick's brother Matty out of the house for being a bad influence on him.

Nick discovers that Matty has been sleeping rough and persuades his dad to let him return home, but Matty is only allowed to do so on the condition that he signs a long list of rules which include no drinking or bringing girls back to the house. Matty breaks these almost immediately – he soon brings Liv back for a noisy sex session. Nick can't stand it and storms out.

The night before his big match, Nick joins the gang at a club. Although he is meant to be staying teetotal in preparation for the game, he starts downing shots. Eventually, after a night of heavy drinking and contemplating, Nick arrives at college and tells an angry rugby team that he is not going to play any more.

His bewildered coach cannot understand his decision, but Nick feels liberated and free and goes home to confront his father. Matty and Nick stand up to their bullying Dad and take control. In a cathartic bonfire they burn the house rules and Nick's rugby clothes.

Nicholas Hoult (Plays Tony Stonem)

It seems that acting came very naturally to 21-year-old Nicholas. At the age of just three his mother took him to the theatre and he sat in the front row. He soon became

NICHOLAS WENT ON TO
BECOME A GLOBAL STAR
AND HAS WORKED WITH
SOME EXCEPTIONAL
ACTORS, INCLUDING THE
DASHING COLIN FIRTH.

engrossed. The director noticed this and told his mum that, if her son was able to concentrate on watching a play at such a young age, he could probably be in one. Consequently, she enrolled Nicholas at the Sylvia Young Theatre School and he made his big-screen debut at the age of seven in *Intimate Relations* alongside Julie Walters.

Directors have often described Nicholas, known to his friends as Nick, as having enormous screen presence, and his slightly unconventional good looks helped him win the part of 12-year-old Marcus in the movie *About A Boy*. Playing opposite global superstar Hugh Grant, Hoult stole the show and received rave reviews for his portrayal of the nerdy and socially inept schoolboy who strikes up an unlikely friendship with a bored, lonely middle-aged man.

He went on to star in Richard E. Grant's semi-biographical movie *Wah Wah* and as Blake in the teenflick *Kidulthood. Kidulthood,* a movie that takes place over 24 hours, is about a bunch of London teenagers and its scenes depicting sex, violence and drugs made it a natural precursor to *Skins.*

Nick was the only well-known actor cast as one of the main characters in the original series of *Skins*, and a lot of pressure was heaped on him to lead the inexperienced actors to victory.

'I knew he was right for the role,' recalls *Skins* creator Bryan Elsey. 'But his performance was far above my wildest expectations. As Tony he gives one of the most shaded and nuanced performances by any actor, young or old that I have ever met.'

From the moment Nick first appeared on screen as the scheming Tony, lying under his now legendary 'naked bodies' duvet cover, teenagers across the country were hooked. Hoult was now a teenage sex symbol, complete with armies of screaming pubescent girls.

Nick appeared to play the heartless heartthrob Tony with ease, but he admits that filming his first sex scenes were embarrassing and terrifying. Not everyone loved Tony either. On occasion teenage boys would abuse him in the street.

'I can see now that perhaps they were jealous or just didn't like character, but if I'm honest it did hurt. I could be walking along, minding my own business and someone would shout 'twat' and then just carry on walking by. Bizarre! I can laugh now but it was very unpleasant at the time.'

'Skins was an amazing experience though,' he recalls, 'I made amazing friends and pissed myself laughing for two years.'

It was also a stepping stone to further Hollywood exposure. He was cast opposite Colin Firth and Julianne Moore in the Oscar nominated *A Single Man* (directed by Tom Ford) and earned a BAFTA Rising Star nomination. 'I was lucky that Tom let me be in it,' adds Nick with self-deprecation. Ford claims that luck had nothing to do with it and it was all down to Nick's talent. 'Nick performs in a way that seems effortless, subtle and honest. He has a maturity and depth that are remarkable.'

During filming Nick picked up a nasty eye injury caused

by ash from the LA bush fires that were raging as they shot. Despite being in a lot of pain, he refused to stop filming which further impressed Ford.

Nick also starred in the blockbuster *Clash of the Titans* and has filmed *X-Men First Class.*

Nina Wadia (plays Bibi Kharral, Anwar's mum)

Bringing the overbearing matriarch of the Massood Family to life in *EastEnders* was a simple stepping-stone for Wadia, as she had played an almost identical role as Anwar's mum Bibi in *Skins* a few years before. In fact, many fans believe the *EastEnders* writers were highly influenced by Anwar and Bibi when they were writing storylines for Wadia's character Zainab and her son Tamwar.

Wadia first caught the public eye in BBC sketch show *Goodness Gracious Me*. She played hilarious Indian stereotypes such as Mrs 'I can make it at home for nothing!' and one half of The Competitive Mothers. She took over from her *Goodness Gracious Me* co-star Meera Syal in the role of Rupinder in the sitcom *All About Me.*

Wadia's comic talents have been well rewarded. She won 'Best Comedy Performance' at the 2009 British Soap Awards and 'Best Onscreen Partnership' at the same awards ceremony for her relationship with Nitin Ganatra.

In 2004 she won the Chairman's Award at the Asian Women awards. Born in 1968 in Mumbai, India, Wadia was schooled in Hong Kong and met her husband in

Nina Wadia.

Canada. They now live on the outskirts of London with their two children.

Novels

With the popularity of *Skins* reaching fever pitch in series three, the creators knew that their fans would be impatient to learn the outcome of their favourite characters in the break between series three and four. The idea of a book to fill in the gap was an excellent one.

In conjunction with publisher Hodder, the first *Skins* novel was published on January 7, 2010. Written by established teen-writer Ali Cronin, *Skins: The Novel* follows the eight main protagonists of series three over the course of the college summer break.

Brand new storylines that did not feature in the following series had fans hooked. Effy flees to Italy where, trying to put her feelings for Freddie and the guilt of attacking Katie out of her mind, she finds the perfect distraction in Aldo, a sophisticated older man.

New lovers Naomi and Emily are missing each other as Emily clashes with sister Katie and struggles to enjoy herself on a family holiday. Although sweetly in love, Thomas and Pandora have not yet had sex, and the three musketeers – Freddy, Cook and JJ – are still are embroiled in a spirited game of sexual one-upmanship.

Like the show, the novel is bursting with raw, authentic narrative, graphic language and sexual scenes. The actors vigorously promoted the book and appeared at signings across the country. Unsurprisingly, thousands of fans stampeded the stores to get a closer look at their idols.

A second novel, *Skins Summer Holiday,* written by Jess Brittain, sister and daughter of co-creators Jamie Brittain and Bryan Elsey, was released in 2011.

Nudity

One of the iconic images of the first series of *Skins* was Tony Stonem's duvet cover, which depicted the life-sized, headless images of a boy and girl in full frontal nudity. Most of the original cast appeared naked at some time, although the boys tended to be more revealing than the girls – particularly Chris, who made big headlines at the time with his scene of total nudity.

O is for...

Ollie Barbeiri (plays JJ Jones)

Cast as JJ at aged 16, Ollie revealed in an interview that he had never had a job in his life, let alone acted. Chosen from 12,000 hopefuls, Ollie had not even been a fan of the show.

'It was all really strange actually. I had never even done a paper round,' he laughed. 'I wasn't actually even that familiar with the show, basically because all my friends liked it and I wanted to be different.

'So before I decided to audition I sat down and watched all the previous episodes and I thought it was brilliant. I was hooked.'

Playing an autistic character is a challenge for any actor, let alone someone with no previous experience, so Ollie made sure he did some research for the character. Also, to

OLLIE HAD NO PREVIOUS ACTING EXPERIENCE BEFORE *SKINS* SO HE HAD DO SOME RESEARCH BEFORE TAKING ON THE ROLE OF JJ.

get in character and form a better understanding of JJ, Ollie dressed the set of JJ's bedroom himself – he made a collage of JJ's friends and how they fitted into his life in an attempt to organise his thoughts. Known as the 'Wall of Friends', director Charles Martin encouraged Ollie to destroy it at the end of shooting his centric episode so that he would understand what it felt like for JJ to be in a destructive rage.

Unusually, a number of the *Skins* production crew made cameo appearances in JJ's centric episode. Assistant Director Seth Adams appeared as a nurse at JJ's therapy clinic, while floor runner Tom Meakin featured in a minor role as a policeman. And the show's location manager appeared in a non-speaking role as a mental patient being pushed in a wheelchair at the psychological clinic.

Ollie, who grew up in Bath, a short distance from Bristol, grew very fond of JJ's character in the two years he played him. He felt his journey from boy to man was one of the show's best pieces of writing. 'Looking solely at JJ's story, it covers everything that a character like that would do in those situations. I think by the end of the series, every base is touched I'm very happy with how he's turned out – he's almost become a friend that I know now!'

Osama! The Musical

Osama! The Musical takes its theme from the events of 9/11. It is the Roundview College drama production that plays a vital part in the plot of the first series. Written by Mr Cathcart, the drama teacher, it stars Maxxie and Michelle in the lead roles, and Sketch helps with the lighting. The production gives Maxxie a chance to demonstrate his considerable dancing and singing abilities. After tricking Michelle out of appearing on the first night by giving her a drug that makes her too ill to perform, Sketch takes over and shows she can also sing and dance with the best of them. But all ends in chaos because gay Maxxie is repelled by Sketch's kiss and tells her so on stage, which earns him a slap. All this is witnessed by Mr Cathcart, who has been fired because Sketch made false allegations about his inappropriate behaviour. However, as the lights go down on opening night, we see Mr Cathcart slip into a seat to witness his masterpiece. Pity for him that it all ends in tears. If you want to hear the music it's all on YouTube.

P

is for...

Pandora Moon (played by Lisa Blackwell)

Pandora, affectionately called Panda by her friends, arrives at Roundview College like a throwback from the fifties. Innocent and immature both in speech and nature, she is nonetheless determined to remedy the situation as quickly as possible. With Effy as her new best friend she doesn't have far to go to find someone to set her a bad example.

Their friendship is an incongruous one. Pandora is full of bubbly, 'jolly hockey sticks' naivety and Effy is sexually promiscuous, secretive and brooding. Yet they complement each other, with Pandora giving Effy more heart and Effy giving Pandora credibility in the 'cool' gang.

When Thomas, an equally naive, spiritual and chivalrous boy from the Congo arrives at Roundview, Pandora –

desperate to have a boyfriend – sets her sights on him immediately. Soon Thomas is thrust into the hedonistic, partying lifestyle of the gang and homesick for Africa. Pandora wants to show him good things about Britain, so invites him round to her Aunt Elizabeth's for tea and scones. They soon discover that her Aunt has been growing huge amounts of cannabis and doesn't know what to do with it all. It just so happens that Thomas is under threat from eviction from his squat by slum landlord and local gangster Johnnie White. Needing to raise £2000 Pandora and Thomas realise they can sell the weed to raise the cash.

Later on, the whole gang go to Thomas's to celebrate. Partying hard with a topless Pandora about to seduce him, Thomas is appalled when his mother and two siblings arrive. Like her son, Thomas's mother is not used to wild teenage ways and she promptly makes him return to the Congo with her.

Pandora is left heartbroken and still a virgin. To cheer herself up she arranges a pyjama party at her house with her seemingly straight-laced mother Angela, played by Sally Phillips. She intends for it to be girls only party where they can watch movies, eat cake and pay twister.

Effy, egged along by the other girls (who include Naomi, Emily and Katie) puts MDMA powder in the cake mix. Angela gets really high and has to take to her bed whilst the girls party on. After Cook and JJ gatecrash the party, Effy and Cook sneak into Angela's wardrobe and discover she has a secret passage into the next house where she has been having S and M sex with her neighbour.

The house descends into chaos. Pandora is upset at the way her friends have treated her and makes them leave. Left alone and missing Thomas, Pandora cannot resist when Cook reappears and offers to take her virginity. The next morning Pandora says goodbye to Cook and guiltily reveals to Effy that she has cheated on Thomas. To Pandora's shock, Thomas appears suddenly and tells her he is staying for good.

Although in love with Thomas, Pandora cannot resist the sexual charms of Cook and continues to have an affair with him. Thomas eventually finds out and the couple split only for them to reunite at the school ball at the end of series three.

Pandora and Thomas have spent a loving summer together when series four begins, but their happy, simple lives are soon shattered when a fellow student commits suicide at a club where Thomas works.

Deeply affected by the incident (and bribed by his boss into keeping quiet to the police that the club was full of underage drinkers), Thomas becomes withdrawn and distant from the gang, taking solace in his local gospel church and prayer group. He is soon attracted to the daughter of the pastor and, after they have sex, he cannot hide his guilty secret from Pandora, who promptly dumps him.

To help get over Thomas, Pandora throws herself into her studies and achieves outstanding results in her exams. She is offered a history scholarship at the world-renowned Harvard University. Unbeknownst to her, Thomas has been scouted for a sports scholarship at Harvard too. When he tells her he is leaving to go to America to study at one of the best universities in the world, Pandora says it's really cool. She doesn't tell Thomas she will be there too, but her knowing smile says it all. They will meet again and reconcile.

Pauline Quirke (plays DS Blunt)

Pauline Quirke, who plays DS Blunt the in-your-face police woman who investigates Sophia's suicide, is often associated with lifelong friend Linda Robson, her co-star in the hit comedy series *Birds of a Feather*. Currently, Pauline is going solo as the character Hazel Rhodes in the ITV soap opera *Emmerdale*.

Pauline began her career as a child when she appeared in *Dixon of Dock Green* as a child of eight. Since then she has appeared in many movies and TV shows. As a teenager, she hosted three children's TV series: *You Must Be Joking, Pauline's Quirkes*, and *Pauline's People*. In 1980, Quirke appeared in the movie *The Elephant Man* along with *Emmerdale* colleague Lesley Dunlop. In 1989, she began playing the part of Sharon Theodopolopodus in *Birds of a Feather* with Linda Robson and Lesley Joseph, and the show made them all household names. In 1996 she starred in the BBC television production of *The Sculptress* and gained a great deal of critical acclaim. The end of *Birds of a Feather* coincided with her landing the title role in the BBC1 drama series *Maisie Raine*. From 2000 to 2003, she

KATE MOLLOY

Pauline Quirke.

Scottish Peter Capaldi plays Sid's father Mark Jenkins.

starred with Warren Clarke in the BBC television series *Down To Earth*. She returned to comedy in 2001 in the BBC sitcom, *Office Gossip*. In 2002, she starred in *Being April*, a comedy drama for BBC One. Since then she has taken the lead in many television drama and series, the most recent role started in May 2010, when it was announced that Quirke would join soap opera *Emmerdale*.

Peter Capaldi (plays Mark Jenkins)

Peter plays Sid's angry and aggressive father Mark Jenkins, who in series one and two finds it hard to relate to his son and is struggling with his marriage break-up.

The multi-talented Scottish actor and film director Peter Capaldi won an Academy Award and a BAFTA award in 1995 for his short film *Franz Kafka's It's a Wonderful Life*. As an actor, he played Oldsen in *Local Hero*, John Frobisher in *Torchwood* and political spin doctor Malcolm Tucker in the British hit TV comedy series *The Thick of It*. Capaldi was born in Glasgow. His mother's family was from County Cavan, Ireland, and his father's from Italy. Capaldi attended Glasgow School of Art. While still at high school, Capaldi was a member of the Antonine Players, who performed at the Fort Theatre, Bishopbriggs. As an art student, Capaldi was the lead singer in the punk rock band Dreamboys. In 2007 Capaldi took the part of Mark Jenkins, Sid's dad, and was killed off in eerie circumstances. Capaldi is best known for his role as spin doctor Malcolm Tucker, in the BBC sitcom *The Thick of It*. The character of Tucker is reputed to be based upon Tony Blair's sometime press secretary Alastair Campbell. In 2006, Capaldi was nominated for the BAFTA and RTS Best Comedy Actor Awards. The movie spin-off from *The Thick of It*, titled *In the Loop*, was released in 2009. He won the 2010 BAFTA Television Award for Male Performance in a Comedy Role. He also won the 2010 British Comedy Award for Best TV Comedy Actor. Since his 1983 appearance as Danny Oldsen in *Local Hero,* Capaldi has appeared in over forty films and television programmes. He starred in Ken Russell's *The Lair of the White Worm* and in Stephen Frears' *Dangerous Liaisons*. He appeared in *Minder* as a dodgy associate of Arthur Daley. He wrote *Hard Top, Soft Shoulder,* winning the Audience Award at the London Film Festival. His first starring role on television was as a closet gay man in the BBC drama series *Mr Wakefield's Crusade*. In ITV's *Prime Suspect 3* he played a transvestite. Capaldi directed the BBC Four sitcom *Getting On*. In 2011 Capaldi won Best TV Comedy Actor at the British Comedy Awards. He lives in Crouch End with his wife, Elaine Collins, and their daughter.

Posh Kenneth (played by Daniel Kaluuya)

Posh Kenneth is a black pupil at Roundview College. He is sometimes seen in the company of the main characters. He often speaks in heavily accented, street-wise, black rapper slang, but when challenged he will sheepishly revert to his

OPPOSITE: DANIEL KALUUYA WHO PLAYS POSH KENNETH HAS GONE ON TO STAR IN SEVERAL FILMS INCLUDING JOHNNY ENGLISH.

real accent, which is educated, and upper-middle class. In the last episode of the first series he shows a romantic interest in Jal, and in the first episode of the second season we see him as a rapper at a party attended by the friends. On the official website, he claims that his ambitions are to be either a politician or a psychiatrist. His heroes are Trevor McDonald and Sigmund Freud. Daniel Kaluuya, who plays Posh Kenneth, recently appeared in the BBC comedy series *Psychoville*. Kaluuya trained at the National Youth Theatre. In an early role he played Reece in the BBC drama *Shoot the Messenger*. As well as acting in the first series of *Skins*, Kaluuya was also a staff writer, and then the head writer on some episodes of the second series. After *Skins*, Kaluuya appeared on television in *Silent Witness*, the Doctor Who special *Planet of the Dead* and *Lewis*. In 2010 he appeared at the Royal Court Theatre in London in his first stage role, in Roy Williams' *Sucker Punch*. He received rave reviews and won both the *Evening Standard* Award and Critics' Circle Theatre Award for Outstanding Newcomer. He is also in the *Johnny English* movie sequel *Johnny English Reborn*.

Q is for...

Quotes

Much of what makes *Skins* so popular and different is the variety of its scripts. There are countless forums dedicated to quotes from *Skins* over the 5 years it has been on air. Here are some of our favourites.

Tony: 'Tonight's the night, Sid. You finally pop the cherry, you finally get the VIP tour of Neverland.'

Michelle to Jal 'Looking good is what I do. You play the clarinet. I look shaggable.'

Cassie: 'I stop eating until they take me to hospital.'

Sid: 'Cassie, I don't care if you think you're odd because when I see you I want to start singing.'

Anwar: 'I'm praying to my God here, Cassie.' Cassie: 'Wow. Can he hear you?' Anwar: 'I hope not, otherwise he'll know about all those pills I necked last night.'

Maxxie: 'I got off with Tony on the Russia trip. I only did it 'cause I fell out with Anwar when he said he hated gays. So I got upset and Tony said he'd give me head to cheer me up, you know? And it didn't mean anything but I lost my head, then he gave me head, then we got deported from Russia and I'm really, really sorry for being a slut, okay?'

Jal: 'The thing about Chris was, he said yes. He said yes to everything. He loved everyone. And he was the bravest boy— man—I knew. He flung himself out of a foil balloon every day. Because he could. Because he was. And that's why—and that's why we loved him.'

Chris: 'Four months without sex that ain't funny. But you probably wouldn't understand that, Jal. You don't have sex at all, do you? You have clarinet lessons.'

JJ: 'I'm JJ. With regard to mathematic aptitude I'm in the top 0.3 per cent of the population which is an interesting demographic statistic because paradoxically my communication interpersonal and intuitive skills are towards the lower quartiles.'

Naomi: 'Hamlet's basically a teenage boy. He's got all these desires, but he doesn't have the bottle to reach out for them. So, he goes mad, and wanks off about Ophelia, and ends up so boring, somebody has to kill him!'

Thomas: I fell in love with this girl... she was good, she was honest... with the doughnuts... Now she's gone, and this new one... I don't like her... she makes my heart hurt.'

Pandora: 'I'm definitely going to have surf and turf *a*sap. Mum says boys only want one thing, so my plan is to give it to them lots of times, get good at it, be really popular, and maybe my toes will stop throbbing.'

Emily: 'I like girls. I like sex with girls. I like their rosy lips, their hard nipples, bums, soft things. I like tits and fanny you know? There, I said it.'

Katie: 'I'm Katie fucking Fitch! Who the fuck are you?

Cook: 'This day's got potential. It's pregnant!'

Freddie: 'I met a girl I like today. She's really beautiful. That's it.'

Effy: 'Sometimes I think I was born backwards, you know came out my mum the wrong way. I hear words go past me backwards. The people I should love I hate, and the people I hate...'

R is for...

Rich Hardbeck (played by Alexander Arnold)

Rich's real passion is heavy metal and he doesn't suffer fools lightly. Swathed in black leather and shrouded by his long, greasy hair, Rich stands out amongst the 'barbies' and 'Cowelheads', as he refers to many of those at Roundview College.

Rich is best friends with Alo, who definitely doesn't share his taste in music or fashion. Alo tells Rich he thinks his style is ruining their chances of finding girlfriends, but Rich refuses to compromise and sets about trying to win the affections of another metalhead who works in the college library. Dubbed the 'angel of death' by Alo, Rich is cruelly rejected by her when he asks her on a date. With a fiercely articulate diatribe she tells Rich she would rather 'lick the shit smeared arsehole of a dead horse with Aids than touch your wiry, gangrenous, vile, inadequate pubescent dick.'

He finds a peculiar comfort in Grace, Mini's über girlie, ballet-loving friend. Despite telling her she is 'everything he despises in a girl,' he feels a strange attraction to her. Grace proves to Rich that there is more to her than hair and make-up and accompanies him to some heavy metal concerts wearing leather and a dog collar. She slamdunks the audience and Rich feels a new admiration for her.

But still confused and feeling rejected by the 'angel of death', Rich heads off to the heavy metal record shop. Toxic Bob, the owner, sells him a rare, £500 record which he describes as 'almost deadly'. Rich plays the music through headphones and sends himself temporarily deaf. Wandering around in a daze, he finds himself at a ballet recital where Grace is performing and –still unable to hear – watches her dance in silence. He is moved by her beauty and grace.

Although a completely incongruous couple, Rich and Grace fall in love.

Ronni Ancona (plays Jenna Fitch, Emily and Katie's mother)

Playing the control freak, homophobic mother of the Fitch twins in series three and four is Ronni Ancona. Born in Troon, Ayrshire, Ronni made an appearance on *Blue Peter*

RONNI ANCONA.

in 1986 while she was still at school. Multi-talented Ronni is an actress, impressionist and author and won the Best TV Comedy Actress award at the 2003 British Comedy Awards for her work in *Big Impression*.

Before *Big Impression*, Ancona had worked in films and TV shows and performed in stand-up comedy. Her comedy career began on the comedy circuit and she won the *Time Out* Hackney Empire New Act of the Year in 1993. In 2005, she co-starred opposite Miranda Richardson and Bill Nighy in *Gideon's Daughter* on BBC One. She was Beline in Molière's *The Hypochondriac* at the Almeida Theatre, has been a guest presenter of *Have I Got News For You*, and also performed on the Channel 4 comedy show *TV Heaven, Telly Hell*. In 2007, the BBC commissioned a new comedy sketch series titled *Ronni Ancona & Co* with Phil Cornwell, Jan Ravens and John Sessions.

In 2009 her first book was published, *A Matter Of Life And Death: How To Wean A Man Off Football*.

Russia

In the first series of *Skins*, an entire episode is devoted to a school trip to Russia. Dramas occur when Tony attempts – unsuccessfully – to seduce Maxxie. Tom Barkley, the History teacher, unsuccessfully attempts to seduce Angie, the psychology teacher, Chris manages to sleep with Angie, and Anwar loses his virginity to a buxom Russian girl (who turns out to be married to a fat, greasy husband who threatens to kill Anwar with a shotgun). Michelle and

Jal go on the pull and get very drunk, cadging drinks from a gang of Russian soldiers. Bribes to placate corrupt Russians have to be paid at every turn, and the grim, crumbling hotel in which they stay looks like something from the Gulag Archipelago.

When the party from Roundview College eventually leave, we see the Russians celebrating the confidence tricks they have played on staff and pupils to get them to part with their money.

S is for...

Sally Phillips (plays Angela Moon, Pandora's mum)

As Pandora's mother Angela, Sally gives a hilarious performance as a seemingly straight-laced parent who enjoys S & M sex on the side. Comedy is in Sally's bones – she got her big break as the non-stop giggling receptionist in *I'm Alan Partridge* and was nominated as the best female newcomer at the British Comedy Awards. She played a starring role in the comedy series *Hippies* and co-created and wrote *Smack the Pony*, the all-female, double Emmy Award-winning comedy show. She also starred in *Bridget Jones's Diary*, playing Bridget's foul-mouthed best friend Jude alongside Hollywood superstars Renée Zellwegger and Hugh Grant. During 2004 and 2009 Sally had recurring parts in the BBC comedies *Jam & Jerusalem* and in the new smash-hit series *Miranda*.

Super smart Sally was born in Hong Kong and graduated from New College, Oxford with a first class degree in Italian. She has also turned her hand to writing – in 2009 she won a British Film Council screenwriting competition for her film *Fag Mountain*.

Sarah Lancashire (plays Mary Miles, Chris's stepmother)

Sarah Lancashire was born in Oldham, Lancashire, and graduated from the Guildhall School of Music and Drama in 1986. She stole the hearts of millions of viewers in her first major role as Raquel, a vulnerable and quirky barmaid in *Coronation Street*. After leaving the soap, Sarah immediately found work in several prestigious television productions. She played Ruth Goddard in the ITV1 drama series *Where The Heart Is*, and appeared with Dawn French in the BBC sitcom *Murder Most Horrid*. In 2005, she starred on the West End stage as Miss Adelaide in the Donmar Warehouse production of *Guys and Dolls*. In the same year, Lancashire made her directorial debut for BBC Radio 4's show *Afternoon Play*, entitled *Viva Las Blackpool*, and was nominated for the Best New Director award at the BAFTAs. She starred in BBC comedy drama *Angel Cake*, and played Mary Miles in *Skins*. She appeared in 'Partners in Crime' in the opening episode of the 2008 series of

SARAH LANCASHIRE.

Doctor Who. Recently, Sarah has starred as Rose in the ITV1 drama series *Rose and Maloney*.

Sean Teale (plays Nick Levan)

Sean excelled at sports at school but decided to switch to acting because it 'looked more fun'. After appearing in a school play two years ago, he was spotted by a talent scout and taken on by a theatrical agent. The agent warned him about playing any contact sports – particularly rugby – for fear the game could harm his looks. Ironically, Sean's *Skins* character Nick is the college jock and captain of the rugby team.

Sean grew up in Putney, London, and attended Latymer Upper School, one of the capital's most prestigious academies. He turned down a role in a short film to concentrate on his studies and did very well in his A Levels, achieving an A and two Bs.

'I turned down the movie, but when my agent told me about the *Skins* auditions I couldn't resist', he told the London Evening Standard. 'It was a stressful time, though, because the auditioning is a long process, over nine weeks, and I kept thinking, either kill me now and let me know I haven't got it so I can pay attention to my exams, or let me know and I can rejoice.'

Sean was told he had got the part just a week into his A Levels and the day before his 18th birthday. Then came the news that he was to be naked in his very first scene. Although scores of female fans will delight in

Sean showing off his hot body he found the nudity very embarrassing.

'I am very different to my character in the way he loves getting his clothes off and I don't. I am not that comfortable in my own skin. It's heart-wrenching watching yourself. But there's nothing more that I enjoy than acting. It doesn't even feel like work.'

He has also enjoyed bringing other aspects of Nick's character to life in the latest series. 'At first Nick seems to be the typical sports hero who is dating the hottest girl in college and appears to have the perfect life,' he reveals.

'But pretty soon we learn that he is actually quite vulnerable and it was good to delve deeper in the character.'

Sebastian De Souza (plays Matty Levan)

Sebastian – who plays the enigmatic Matty in the third generation of *Skins* – grew up with the arts and discovered his love of theatre at a young age. His father Chris De Souza is a broadcaster and composer and Sebastian himself is a talented pianist and clarinettist – he was 13 -years- old when he won a music scholarship to St Edward's School, Oxford. Also excelling at drama, Sebastian played Puck in *A Midsummer Night's Dream*, took the lead role of Pip in *Great Expectations* and even played the title character in Shakespeare's *Henry V*. At 16, Sebastian joined the National Youth Theatre and was taken on by a theatrical agent in 2009.

Sebastian grew up in Boxford, near Newbury, and was

the last of the third generation characters to be cast. 'My character was cast a week after everybody else,' he revealed to entertainment website Digital Spy. 'At the final audition, there are only usually about two people, but there were five at mine so it was nerve-wracking.

'Because *Skins* is such a raw and realistic representation of being a teenager the casting agents expect you to come along and be yourself. They cast you on who you are as a person. I'm not very similar to my character but I think there are qualities in me that I share with him.'

Sebastian intends to continue his A Level studies and is hoping to cope well with the huge amount of attention *Skins* is bound to bring him and is determined to stay level-headed.

'Although I feel this is a fantastic acting opportunity and I am very grateful to be playing Matty, it is very important that I don't cruise along in my education. I have done that in the past but now I want to prove to myself that I'm able to get really good grades and give a really good performance on television.' He adds, 'I feel comfortable on stage – perhaps it's possibly an inadequacy in myself that I feel more comfortable playing someone else.'

Matty is also a talented singer and songwriter and loves to perform his songs in front of an audience.

Sid Jenkins (played by Mike Bailey)

At first, Sid is portrayed as a loser with low self-esteem – a nice enough guy, but still a virgin and always unlucky with girls. His best friend, Tony Stonem, whose instructions he tends to follow without question, manipulates Sid like a puppet and treats him with cheerful contempt.

Sid is hopelessly in love with Tony's girlfriend Michelle. Tony knows it, but it causes him no concern – he uses this knowledge to play control games with both of them. In most ways, Sid is a disaster. When we first meet him he is masturbating in bed when he is interrupted by a call from Tony. The scene immediately establishes the nature of the relationship. Tony meets him in a greasy spoon cafe where Sid is eating his usual meal of junk food. Tony instructs him to go a drug dealer's headquarters in a nearby suburban brothel in order to buy an ounce of spliff for the party they will attend that night. Tony's plan is for them to buy the spliff on credit, keep enough for their own consumption, and sell the rest to the other partygoers in order to pay for it. But Sid fall fouls of the drug dealer, Mad Twatter, an insane character with a vast handlebar moustache. Bullied and terrified by Twatter, he has three times the amount he requested of the drug forced upon him and is landed with a massive debt. When he is accused of being a 'fuck up' he wearily acknowledges the truth of the statement. Made miserable by his own ineptitude and his infatuation with Michelle, he fails to appreciate Cassie, who has been provided by Michelle on Tony's instigation so that Sid can lose his virginity. Sid is so introverted by his own failure, he fails to see how wounding his indifference towards Cassie is – she is in a fragile mental state, as she suffers from anorexia nervosa and low self-esteem.

In the second series, Tony is recovering from brain damage following a road accident. We learn that, when Tony was in a coma, Sid attended the hospital and read books to the unconscious Tony. But gradually Sid drifts away and frees himself from Tony's manipulative influence, and begins to develop a stronger personality of his own.

Gone are the days when he was beaten up by Jal's brother and peed on by a dog and a vagrant while he lay in the gutter. Since Tony's brain injuries, a stronger, more independent Sid has emerged, and Tony has also changed into someone quite unlike the confident, vain, self-obsessed character we first met. Despite his many faults, Sid is always loyal to his friends and Cassie finds him lovable, even though he takes so long to respond to her affections. Despite his growing independence from Tony, Sid remains a bespectacled, shambling figure in hideous clothes. Sid is intelligent, but unlike Tony (who before his accident is outstandingly brilliant) Sid never measures up to his true abilities as he is unable to apply himself. Although Sid is portrayed as a constant loser, he is reckoned to be the audience's favourite character in series one and two. Sid is a universal character who encapsulates the same anxieties, doubts, lack of self-esteem, and fear of the future that make up the common experience of most teenagers.

Although he is constantly the butt of his Scottish father's rage, and consequently seen as weak, Sid eventually proves himself to have reserves of strength and resolve. When Sid's father, Mark Jenkins, cannot prevent Sid's mother from leaving him, Sid reveals the depths of his own rage at her leaving and this is exacerbated because he has been on the receiving end of his father's anger for so long. Ironically, Sid's sudden anger improves his relationship with his father because it shows Mark how to stand up to his own bullying father and forces him to sort out of his life. Because Sid is on a journey of development and self-discovery, his relationship with Cassie is ever changing but her character remains constant. The audience discovers, at the same time Sid does, that despite her troubled psychiatric past he loves Cassie.

Things take a turn for the worse for Sid when the menacing figure of Madison Twatter, to whom Sid owes money for drugs becomes a substitute teacher at the school. Eventually Madison corners Sid and Jal and, to demonstrate his viciousness, smashes Jal's clarinet as a warning to Sid about his unpaid drug debt. When Tony offers Sid the opportunity to date Michelle, he takes it but when he gets home he finds Cassie waiting. She is upset that he has stood her up. She tries to be positive, but is wounded that Michelle has Sid's love without ever having earned it.

After Tony encourages Sid to think that he can win Michelle, he takes her back in front of Sid, thus demonstrating the power he has over both of them. Distraught by Sid's cancelling of their date, Cassie takes an overdose and is taken to hospital. Jal accompanies her, and Jal places the blame on Sid. Later, on a school trip to Russia, he sees a picture of Cassie that Maxxie has drawn and says how beautiful he has made her look. Finally, Sid realises he really wants Cassie. But, on the rebound after splitting with Tony, Michelle offers to have sex with him. At this point, Sid realises that his affection for Michelle is no stronger than friendship. Cassie is sent to a recovery clinic in Scotland and they communicate by a visual computer link. Sid sees Cassie in what he interprets as a compromising situation with another man. In reality, the man is only Cassie's gay friend. Sid accuses Cassie of cheating on him and destroys the laptop he used to communicate with her.

A visit from Sid's monstrously selfish grandfather, uncle and cousins explains why Sid's dad feels crushed by life. Finally, he stands up to his own father and throws him out, but the stress proves too much and he dies. His body is discovered by Sid the next morning. Still in shock, Sid can do nothing except leave his dad's body in the house. He goes to college as usual but finally breaks down in front of Tony. With Tony's support, the two of them go back to Sid's house to deal with the situation. This incident seems to patch up their damaged friendship. Finally, Sid takes a train to Scotland in order to see Cassie. However, at the same Cassie takes a train in the opposite direction, presumably to visit Sid in Bristol.

Michelle organises a camping trip to celebrate her birthday, but Tony is excluded. Sid, still grieving over his dad's death and separated from Cassie, ends up having sex with Michelle (who has given up on Tony) on the beach. They decide to keep their new relationship a secret. But after the camping trip, Cassie, who has returned from

Scotland, catches Sid and Michelle kissing. Later, after running into the couple at a club, Cassie angrily confronts Sid and Michelle in front of their friends. This also exposes Sid and Michelle's new relationship to Tony, who seems hurt by it. Sid attempts to explain things, but Cassie slaps him, telling him he can't do whatever he wants just because his father is dead.

In the episode 'Tony', Sid goes with Michelle to try and make amends with Tony. After coming back from a university interview, Tony finds Sid and Michelle having sex in the toilets of a club. He tells them he loves them both, and even kisses Sid, saying he loves him even though he's a 'useless fucker'. He also tells Sid that he neither loves nor belongs with Michelle – Tony thinks Sid belongs with Cassie. But Sid's relationship with Cassie still proves strewn with difficulties. However, help is on the way. Sid helps Effy with her schoolwork and in exchange she sets out to 'sort out his fucking soap opera'. Effy takes pictures of Cassie kissing another boy and emails them to Sid. Distraught, Sid goes to Cassie's house and the two are reunited.

In the series two finale, Sid is told by Chris's dad that the gang cannot attend Chris' funeral because their degenerate behaviour and drug taking has brought about his death. As a consequence of the ban, Sid and Tony steal Chris's coffin to give him a funeral of their own, but return it at Jal and Michelle's demand. In a final act of kindness, Tony presents Sid with a ticket to New York to find Cassie, who fled there to cope with her grief at Chris's death. Tony hugs Sid, advises him to lose the hat as it 'makes [him] look retarded'

MIKE (SID) WITH HIS CO-STARS LARISSA (JAL) AND KAYA (EFFY) ENJOYING THE LIMELIGHT.

and says that he has always loved him best. Later, we see Sid putting on his hat again, thus proving that he is still friends with Tony, but finally independent of him too. Sid arrives in New York with a photograph of Cassie and walks the streets showing Cassie's picture to passing strangers. He walks past the restaurant where she is working, but then turns back. We now know he will find her again.

Simon Day (plays Leo McLair)

As Freddie and Karen's widower father, Leo has to be both mum and dad to his two tear-away offspring. Simon Day captures the fragility of Leo's character beautifully, leading the audience to empathise with his plight – he is constantly hoovering and cooking, desperately trying to hold the family together after the suicide of his wife, who suffered from psychotic depression. The role is quite a departure for Day, best known for his comedy roles in *The Fast Show* and its spin-off *Swiss Toni*.

Having trained at the Bristol Old Vic, Day's stand-up comedy won him the 1991 Time Out Newcomer of the Year. He came to the attention of Vic Reeves and Bob Mortimer, starred in two series of their *Big Night Out* and continued to work with Reeves throughout the nineties.

In *The Fast Show*, Day's most memorable sketches centred on his characterisations of Competitive Dad – an odious parent constantly trying to beat his children at various sports and games of intellect – and Geoff, the alcoholic car salesman sidekick of Swiss Toni.

Siwan Morris (plays Angie)

Born in Glynneath, Wales, Siwan speaks Welsh and English. She was educated in South Wales and is a graduate of Manchester Metropolitan University. She has appeared in the S4C television programme *Caerdydd,* and acted occasionally in *Casualty* as well as taking a variety of parts with the Royal Shakespeare Company. She played Angie in series one of *Skins* and appeared briefly in the second series. She played Llinos in the Welsh language TV series *Con Passionate,* Liv Jones in the BBC Wales drama *Belonging,* and also appeared in the TV series *Mine All Mine.* As a singer, she has worked with Welsh electropop band Clinigol, and was a guest vocalist on their debut album.

Sketch (played by Aimee-Ffion Edwards)

Sketch is a Welsh girl at Roundview College who is both delusional and obsessive. She lives in the same group of high rise council flats as Maxxie, on whom she has become disturbingly focused.

Sketch's bedridden mother suffers from multiple sclerosis and Sketch harbours a deep-seated anger towards her because she feels she has never been properly looked after during her childhood. Suffering from low self-esteem, Sketch doesn't connect with other teenagers. But, to her, Maxxie is someone who can make her life complete. She tells her mother they are in love, when in fact, her only connection to Maxxie is through taking photographs of him from a distance and sticking them on her wall.

Knowing Maxxie is gay, Sketch tries to make herself more appealing to him by wearing men's clothes and binding her chest with a sash to flatten her breasts. In her efforts to win Maxxie, she proves herself to be clever and manipulative with no concern for the damage she may do to others. She is depicted as a pathological stalker whose obsession about becoming Maxxie's girlfriend leads into her putting others in danger. Sketch works on the lighting for the musical production of *Osama! The Musical*, the school production, which Maxxie and Michelle star in as the lead players. It is directed by Mr Gelcart, the drama teacher. Sketch drops a light from the rafters when she sees Michelle kissing Maxxie as part of her role. Luckily it narrowly misses Michelle. Later, Sketch goes to a party held by Mr Gelcart where she pleads with him to give her Michelle's part. Gelcart scoffs at the suggestion, and in revenge she reports him to the head teacher, saying he kissed and rubbed against her. He is fired as a result. That evening Maxxie asks Sketch out on a date. Initially she is utterly delighted, believing all her dreams have come true, but is quickly disillusioned when she learns Maxxie is asking for Anwar not himself.

Later, Sketch becomes friendly with Michelle, who shares her disdain for men. Sketch pretends to be her friend and because she is obsessed with Maxxie she can barely think straight and breaks into Maxxie's home, and masturbates on his bed. Maxxie arrives back after a party, and Sketch hides for the night under his bed. Later, Maxxie finds a distinctive red hair clip on the floor in his bedroom and realises that Sketch is stalking him when he sees her wearing a matching hair clip. He calls at her flat, where he discovers that Sketch has told her mother that he is her boyfriend. On discovering the truth about her daughter's obsession, Sketch's mother realises Sketch has lied about Mr Gelcart's assault. When she threatens to reveal this, Sketch ties her to the bed so she cannot make any phone calls and heads off to college for the play.

In order to take over Michelle's starring role in the school musical, Sketch gives Michelle some pills, claiming they will settle her first night nerves. Instead they make Michelle continually throw up. Sketch is given Michelle's part, which she has understudied. In the role, she and Maxxie kiss, but he is enraged by her obsession with him. At the moment of their kiss, Maxxie whispers to her that he 'felt nothing' and that she disgusts him. Sketch slaps him on stage – much to the bewilderment of the audience – and Maxxie yells at her until she walks off. The play ends abruptly, leaving the audience confused.

Sketch goes home, gets rid of the boyish clothes she wears, and heads out to Anwar's house. Once there, she claims that she has always fancied him. They have sex, but Sketch looks at a photograph of Maxxie while it takes place – evidently, her obsession for Maxxie is not over.

Sketch apologises for what she has done in the past and tells Maxxie that she is over him and she now likes Anwar. However, during a singsong over the campfire for Michelle's birthday, she sings *If You're Not The One* and stares at Maxxie intensely as she perform the song. It is obvious that she still is suffering from the same infatuation.

Sketch and Maxxie bump into each other at a house party held by Chris. The pair are still hostile even though she insists she is over him. Meanwhile, Sketch has persuaded Anwar to dye his hair and dress exactly like Maxxie. After talking to Maxxie, Anwar realises that Sketch is turning him into a clone and decides to dump her.

Sketch tries to convince Anwar that he has no future and that his friends will move on without him. She wants Anwar to stay with her as she intends to be a full time carer for her mother. But Anwar is invited to share a flat with Maxxie and his new partner in London. He goes with them, leaving Sketch behind.

Skins Parties

Given the hard-hitting storylines and sexual content of *Skins*, it is easy to see why the programme constantly hits the headlines. But *Skins* is one of the shows that can lay claim to having coined a phrase. The term '*Skins* Parties' was seized upon by the media to describe nights of teenage debauchery and drunkenness and a rise in out-of-control parties that required police intervention.

According to press reports, a teenage girl threw a party in County Durham during the 2007 Easter Holidays and advertised it on Myspace as a '*Skins* Unofficial Party'. This was in reference to the series trailer which bore the headline 'Let's trash the average-sized house party'. Her parents were horrified when more than 200 people turned up causing over £20,000 worth of damage. The remorseful young girl claimed her Myspace account had been hacked and that someone else had posted the ad. The incident made national newspaper headlines all over the country and countless similar stories have been reported. Today, any out of control teenage get together is referred to in the press as a '*Skins* Party'.

T is for...

Thomas Tomone (played by Merveille Lukeba)

We do not meet Thomas until the third episode of series three when, having just arrived from the Congo, he is portrayed as very much an innocent abroad. In stark contrast to most of the *Skins* gang, particularly Cook, Effy and Katie, Thomas is gentle, chivalrous and sexually inexperienced. Attempting to make a better life for his family – who are to join him in a few days – Thomas is at first taken aback by the fast pace and rudeness he encounters in the UK. He finds an empty, squalid flat in a council estate and decides to squat there. Hating injustice, Thomas fights off some thuggish boys who are terrorising a newsagent. In return for his help, the newsagent gives

Thomas a box of doughnuts which he begins to devour whilst sitting at a bus stop. Effy and Pandora are also waiting for the bus and Thomas offers them some of his tasty treats. Effy refuses, but Pandora polishes the rest off before being violently sick. Ever the gentleman, Thomas helps Pandora home and there is a sparkle of attraction between them.

His warm English welcome from Pandora is soon shattered when local gangster Johnnie White arrives with his minions at Thomas's flat. They claim to run the estate and demand Thomas pay extortionate rent or face eviction. To prove how hard he is, Johnnie drinks a piping hot Pot Noodle down in one.

Homesick and lonely, Thomas obtains a job at Roundview College and Pandora finds him near to tears whilst watching an African dance class. Knowing he has a sweet tooth, she invites him to her Aunt Elizabeth's for tea and scones to cheer him up. Once there, they discover that Aunt Elizabeth has been growing cannabis and has so much she doesn't know what to do with it. Realising he can sell it to pay off Johnnie White, Thomas and the gang head to the local nightclub to find buyers.

While Thomas is doing a roaring trade, enjoying the nightlife and getting closer to the gang, Johnnie White watched from the shadows, furious that Thomas is selling drugs on what he considers to be his turf. Johnnie challenges Thomas to a winner-takes-all duel. Producing a huge bowl of super-spicy chillies, he declares whoever can eat the most will win the duel, the cash and the use of the flat.

Taking a huge handful, Thomas eats the chillies with relish. Johnnie attempts to match him, but cannot take the heat and begins to splutter and cough. His face reddens and eventually he has a very nasty accident in his trousers.

Victorious, the gang head back to Thomas's and a wild party kicks off. Pandora and Thomas are ready to consummate their relationship and are rolling around in their underwear when Thomas's mother Kosoke arrives unexpectedly. Horrified by her son's lifestyle, she drags him promptly back to the Congo.

Heartbroken, and believing she will never see Thomas again, Pandora turns to Cook to take her virginity, but is riddled with guilt when Thomas returns to Bristol, determined to make a better life for his family.

All is well until Cook takes some of JJ's medicine and admits that he is still sleeping with Pandora. Thomas overhears him and is shattered. He tries to forgive Pandora but he cannot control his anger – he lashes out at Cook while on a camping trip, and dumps Pandora.

Thomas and Pandora make up by the end of series three, but there is trouble ahead. In the first episode of series four, Thomas is the DJ at a nightclub when Sophia, a local Army Cadet commits suicide while high on MDMA.

Shaken by the incident, Thomas is sickened further when the nightclub owner tries to buy his silence (the girl was an underage drinker) with a bribe. Knowing how much his family need the money, Thomas takes the cash with a very heavy conscience and to make matters worse he is expelled from Roundview for bringing the college into disrepute and his mother is ashamed of him for taking the money.

With his life falling apart, Thomas feels distant from Pandora and his friend's frivolous lifestyles. He seeks solace at his local African prayer group. He soon becomes attracted to Andrea, the daughter of the parish pastor who comforts him after his little brother is hospitalised with a lung infection. Thomas tells his mother they must move from the damp, squalid flat because it is unhealthy, but she berates him for challenging her parenting technique. Overcome with anguish and despair at his calamitous life, he cannot resist having sex with Andrea in the hospital laundry room.

Because Thomas is such a decent guy, he admits his infidelity to Pandora. But, despite having done the same thing with Cook, she dumps him. He does not pursue a relationship with Andrea. Pandora is the one he loves and no matter what, he cannot stop loving her.

He uses the bribe money as a deposit on a house and gets a job at a confectionary warehouse to support his family. However, he continues to be rebuffed and ostracised by Pandora – even though she still loves him, her pride gets in the way, and she refuses to take him back.

Helping others out is what Thomas does best. Growing closer to JJ, he helps him to win the heart of a pretty colleague. He also listens to Katie when she tells him of her premature menopause and makes her feel special and strong. In return, Katie resolves to help him win Pandora back.

In the final episode, after throwing himself into fitness training, super-fast sprinter Thomas catches the eye of a sports coach who helps him win an athletics scholarship to Harvard University in the USA. What he doesn't know is that Pandora is off to Harvard too and the audience is left feeling sure the lovers will reconcile.

Tony Stonem (played by Nicholas Hoult)

Tony Stonem, portrayed by Nicholas Hoult, is the most complex character in the first generation of *Skins*. He appears to suffer none of the emotional problems that plague most teenagers. Confident in his good looks and proud of his superior intellectual powers, he compares the lives of those around him to the functions of subatomic particles. Life presents no problems for Tony – his only desire is to gratify his physical desires and explore his philosophical needs. Tony is the archetypal anti-hero. Some of his behaviour and machinations are repellent. Physically, he is extremely attractive, and he is loved by Michelle, who puts aside her powerful personality in order to grant Tony his every

TONY IS PLAYED BY THE INCREDIBLE ACTOR NICHOLAS HOLT.

whim. His best friend is the hapless Sid, who is everything Tony is not – unsure of himself, a bit of a slob, and deeply dissatisfied with still being a virgin. He allows Tony to dominate his life, and goes along with his every suggestion. Tony's relationship with his family is interesting. His mother is unhappily married to his father, and appears to be nothing but a cipher, married to a foul-mouthed and ineffectual husband. Tony's dad has nothing in common with his son and Tony treats him with amiable contempt and plays tricks on him for his own amusement. His relationship with Effy, his beautiful young, wild-child sister is different. He is protective of her and very affectionate. Although Tony is portrayed as a bisexual, it is never made clear if this is his true sexual orientation or simply intellectual curiosity. The depths of his intellectual beliefs are never stated in conversation, but clues are provided in the books we see him reading at various times in the first and second series. Tony's character undergoes a major change in the second series as a result of brain damage caused by a road accident that gives him a subdural haematoma. Not only is he physically handicapped, but he has also lost his greater powers of intelligence along with his libido. After the accident, Tony is suddenly more vulnerable than his friends, a situation that allows them to emerge from the stifling dominance of his personality and develop their own characters.

Tony's sexual conquests are many. Jal can recite a long list of his encounters. At one point, Michelle says to Abigail that he 'fucks everyone, including boys'. On a school trip to Russia, Tony attempts to perform oral sex on Maxxie, saying he wants to 'to try something new'. In a psychology lesson, he equates sex with power. Tony's books reveal his inner self. At various times we see him reading *La Nausée* (Nausea) by Jean-Paul Sartre – a novel about the philosophy of existentialism and self-definition – and Friedrich Nietzsche's *Thus Spoke Zarathustra*, which challenges existing moral values. He also reads Jeanette Winterson's *Oranges Are Not the Only Fruit*, a book about a young girl struggling to come to terms with her homosexuality, and Ayn Rand's *Atlas Shrugged*, in which the author upholds the right for gifted and exceptional people to rise above the demands of the common herd.

Tony connives for Michelle to introduce her friend Cassie to Sid so that he can lose his virginity. Tony does this not for Sid's sake, but because he doesn't want to be associated with a loser. He also orders Sid to acquire some weed on credit from local drug dealer Madison Twatter, which puts Sid in danger. Eventually, Tony ends up driving a stolen car with his friends into the harbour where the drugs are lost.

Tony begins a relationship with local rich girl Abigail. He uses her to break up with Michelle, claiming that he is doing it for Sid, to give him an opportunity to pursue his crush on Michelle. But then Tony gets back with Michelle, seemingly in an attempt to emotionally damage Sid.

Michelle is shocked to observe Tony attempting to have oral sex with Maxxie, and starts to believe he could be a closet homosexual. Later, Michelle watches Tony flirting with Maxxie. Furiously angry at his behaviour, she punches Tony as a prelude to dumping him.

Michelle starts a relationship with Abigail's brother, Josh, causing a jealous Tony to scheme to get her back. He takes explicit sexual pictures of Abigail, and then transfers them to Josh's phone, which he has stolen. He sends the images to Michelle from Josh's phone in order to make her think Josh is in a sexual relationship with his own sister. Tony attempts reconciliation with Michelle, but she turns him down.

Eventually, Tony faces up to the troubles caused by his manipulative nature when his sister Effy is abducted by Josh and drugged. Josh captures Tony and he is presented with a terrible situation. Josh says Tony must have sex with his unconscious sister if he wants to release her from her captors. This scares Tony so much that Josh considers his fear as punishment enough. Satisfied by Tony's humiliation, Josh thinks that a lesson has been learned and he lets him go. Tony's friendship with Sid recovers because Sid was the only one to stand by him in his search for Effy. Tony eventually repays Sid by getting him out of the mental wing of the rehab clinic (Sid was put in a strait-jacket after trying to find Cassie, who he believed was incarcerated at the clinic).

Tony tries to call Michelle on the night of Anwar's party, but loses the signal on his mobile. He stands in the middle of the road to get the signal back and tell Michelle that he really does love her. The conversation comes to an abrupt end because he is knocked down. Michelle is left gazing at her phone, as Effy, in shock, cradles Tony's body.

Later, in series two, after suffering from a subdural haematoma, Tony is totally changed by his accident. He is no longer a sharp-witted, confident character. When talking to Maxxie's mum he says 'I'm stupid now'. Among his general disabilities he has lost the control of his hand that enables him to write. Maxxie eventually helps him scrawl his name.

Suffering from memory loss, Tony gradually begins to recall his feelings for Michelle, but the results of his accident keep the relationship from developing further. They attempt sex, but Tony has also become impotent.

After the school musical (when Michelle does not appear on the stage because Sketch has given her an emetic that makes her continually vomit) Tony finds Michelle and tells her he recalls he told her that he loved her the night of his accident.

Michelle perseveres with Tony and attempts to seduce him again, despite protests from Tony's mother. Michelle fails as Tony is still having sexual problems. She is deeply upset that Tony cannot respond to her advances and leaves, saying she needs more time. Tony decides not to go with the rest of the gang on Michelle's birthday camping trip, but still gets her a present. On the trip Michelle has sex on the beach with Sid, who is still grieving for his father. Afterwards, Michelle opens Tony's birthday present.

She finds that it is her watch, which Tony had been

wearing when his accident took place. There is a note from Tony enclosed: 'You said you needed some time'.

Tony continues to recover but he is still not totally in command of his speech patterns. However, he helps Sid come to terms with his father's unexpected death and starts learning to swim again. He talks to Chris and claims he will 'get everything back again', including Michelle. He is disgusted when finding out Sid and Michelle have become a couple and are having sex.

Tony tries to return to his old lifestyle, taking drugs and going to clubs. Cassie gives him an ecstasy pill, and Tony confronts Sid and Michelle sarcastically to say how happy he is for them. Then he begins to react badly to the drugs and has a panic attack in the toilets.

Strange things begin to happen to Tony. A mysterious girl approaches him. She reveals all sorts of details from his personal life, despite them never having met before. Later, he takes a train to a university open day. On the train, Tony falls into conversation with a soldier who has visible disfiguring burns on his face. The man tells Tony the story of how he came to receive them. At the University, he attends a group interview conducted by the same man he met on the train, but he no longer has the disfiguring burns. We begin to realise that we are observing hallucinations suffered by Tony.

The mysterious girl is also at the meeting and attacks the head of the university with scathing effect. After being ejected from the interview, Tony and the girl embark on a spree of misbehaviour that continues throughout the day.

The viewer realises that the girl may be a figment of Tony's imagination — she teaches him how to swim again, but as the camera pans back we see he is swimming alone. Later, Tony is introduced to her two promiscuous flatmates, who she says gave her a distinctive tattoo. Tony and the girl have sex, demonstrating Tony has regained his lost sexual libido. Eventually we see the tattoo on the girl's back is actually on Tony's and we realise the girl has actually been a creation of Tony's subconscious.

Tony is also shown to have regained his confidence and intelligence. He finds Sid and Michelle and tells them that he loves them both but says he disapproves of their sexual relationship. Finally, Tony receives better A Levels than all his friends. He has passed with three As and a B.

In the end, Tony is set to go to Cardiff University. He gives a ticket to Sid so that he can go and find Cassie in New York. As Sid leaves, Tony is unable to hold back his tears.

At the end of the episode, Tony and Michelle discuss their relationship, but it is not made clear if they will stay lovers, as they are to attend different universities.

Tours

On the back of the phenomenal success of *Skins*, Channel 4 launched a series of rollicking music tours around the country to introduce new live acts and give the public a chance to party with the stars of the show.

In January 2011, tickets sold out almost immediately as

the tour visited all eight of the hometowns of the main characters of the Third Generation. Kicking off in Bristol, the tour (which featured Katy B, The Wombats, Morning Parade and Kissy Sell Out) pumped up the volume and was a smash hit in Swansea, Hereford, Ashford, Edinburgh, London, Brighton and Oxford.

For those who missed out on tickets, the official *Skins* website has a link to photographs and videos of the events.

Twins

Real life identical twins Megan and Kathryn Prescott take the roles of the Fitch sisters in the second generation of *Skins*. In the series, Katie – played by Megan – is six minutes older than Emily – played by Kathryn – but in real life it is the other way round.

Jamie Brittain, co-creator and head writer on the show, reveals that the twins were the very first idea the production team had for the second generation of characters.

To distinguish between the two, the show's stylist Kirstie Stanway began experimenting with different hairstyles and make-up. Although their personalities in the show are quite different, at first it was incredibly hard to tell them apart because they are uncannily alike. By series four, Emily had dyed her hair red and Katie was wearing Chanel-inspired suits, which made things much easier.

Before *Skins*, Kathryn had far more acting experience than her sister Megan, but the writers were very impressed with how Megan portrayed Katie and gave her more depth in series four.

A special twin language was also introduced to the show to depict a real life phenomenon only shared by twins. In times of trouble Emily and Katie speak in 'twin', a language they invented that is only comprehensible to them.

About 40 per cent of twins will develop some form of autonomous language, using nicknames, gestures, abbreviations or terminology exclusively with each other. The technical term for twin language is 'cryptophasia'.

U is for...

USA Version

Premiering on Jan 17, 2011, the US version of *Skins* hit the screens of MTV and caused an almighty row. From day one, the show (set in Baltimore instead of Bristol) made headlines across the US amid calls for it to be banned.

Following the show's premiere, the Parents Television Council called *Skins,* 'the most dangerous show for children we have ever seen'. The council then called for a federal investigation into whether the show violates child pornography and exploitation laws.

Pretty soon big advertisers such as Taco Bell, General Motors, Wrigley and Subway pulled their commercial backing for the show, which lead creator Bryan Elsey to make a detailed statement released by MTV.

DANNY FLAHERTY, SOFIA BLACK-D'ELIA AND JAMES NEWMAN WERE CAST TO STAR IN THE US VERSION OF *SKINS*.

Defending the show he said:

> *Skins* is a very simple and in fact rather old-fashioned
> television series. It's about the lives and loves of
> teenagers, how they get through high school, how
> they deal with their friends, and also how they
> circumnavigate some of the complications of sex,
> relationships, educations, parents, drugs and alcohol.
> The show is written from the perspective of
> teenagers, reflects their world view, and this has caused
> a degree of controversy both in the UK and the USA.
>
> In the UK, viewers and commentators very quickly
> realised that although there are some sensational
> aspects to the show, *Skins* is actually a very serious
> attempt to get to the roots of young people's lives. It
> deals with relationships, parents, death, illness, mental
> health issues, the consequences of drug use and sexual
> activity. It is just that these are characterised from the
> point of view of the many young people who write
> the show and has a very straightforward approach to
> their experiences; it tries to tell the truth. Sometimes
> that truth can be a little painful to adults and parents.

As with the original series, the US version features a cast of
amateur actors and young writers. The first episode was
almost identical to the original – barring the changing of
some names and the replacement of gay dancer Maxxie
with a lesbian cheerleader called Tea.

Esley revealed that he was first approached about a US

adaptation as far back as 2009 but initially felt it wouldn't work. He was approached by various cable networks and eventually felt that MTV had the clearest vision.

'The other networks were missing a commitment to the core values of the show,' he added. 'MTV were clearly taking a risk and they were prepared to take that risk.'

The next challenge was to find the right writers. 'We started at the top of the Hollywood tree and worked our way down,' revealed Elsey. 'It wasn't until we got to the bottom that we actually found writers we liked. We started saying to agents, "Who have you just taken on? Who's got a great play on somewhere?" And that turned up just incredible writers that have never done anything in the mainstream.'

As with the UK version, virtual unknowns were cast as the main characters, with open casting calls held in Toronto and New York City. Six of the nine main cast members have never acted before. Elsley adds, 'It was very important to us that the kids are not seasoned professionals. The cast is made up of:

BRITNE OLDFORD

Britne, 18, and very recently graduated from high school, is playing the mixed-up and fragile Cadie, who is based on Cassie from the first UK show. Portrayed as a pill popper and anorexic, Cadie is a tough part to play convincingly as she is a complex character with many strengths and weaknesses. Britne only heard about the Toronto open audition a couple of hours beforehand and very nearly didn't make it. This is her first TV role and she is combining it with college, where she is studying theatre and vocal performance. Britne also has an interesting talent for playing the ukulele.

CAMILLE CRESENCIA-MILLS

Cast as Daisy (based on goody two-shoes Jal), Camille is also from Toronto and was born in July 1993. She still lives at home with her mum

BRITNE OLDFORD.

and dad and is a student at Etobicoke School of the Arts. Camille has some acting experience including parts in US sci-fi hit *Warehouse 13* and the internet series *Motherload*. Camille has also studied jazz and ballet and is a keen dancer in her spare time. Like her character, she loves to get lost in a good book.

DANIEL FLAHERTY

One of the most experienced members of the cast is Daniel, who plays Tony's hapless sidekick Stanley (based on the role of Sid). Just 18-years-old, Daniel has already appeared in 11 movies. He is also a keen Shakespearean player and has taken roles with The Reduced Shakespeare Company as well as several plays for Glen Rock High School and Bergen Community College in New Jersey.

Daniel trained at NuStars in New York, and also plays the lead guitar for a garage band, writes his own songs and enjoys creating and editing film.

JAMES NEWMAN

Making his acting debut as Tony is James Newman. Like his British counterpart, Tony is a control freak who manipulates his friends and rules their lives. Fans of the US show have even referred to him as a sociopath. But if the storylines continue to reflect the British version, they will find out that he is human underneath.

JAMES NEWMAN.

James was urged to audition for the show by his older brother, but missed the first auditions. Luckily for him, the producers held some more, which he attended!

JESSE CARERE

Jesse Carere hooked up with Ron Mustafaa and Britne Oldford at the open audition because they thought he would be perfect for the part of Chris. They advised him to just be himself and their advice worked.

Jesse, from Toronto, got the news he had the part on Christmas Eve and said it was the best present he could possibly have asked for. Before the audition he was unemployed – although he had always wanted to act, he didn't think he could afford to. It was his sister who gave him the flyer for the audition and he says he will be forever grateful.

RACHEL THEVENARD

Playing Michelle, Tony's beautiful but long-suffering girlfriend is a brand new experience for Rachel, a native of Waterloo, Ontario. She is relatively new to acting but has been involved with Waterlook Youth Theatre for some time. She is a fanatical tweeter and follows 50 Cent avidly.

RON MUSTAFAA

Taking on the role of Abbud is Ron Mustafaa. Abbud is based on the original character of Anwar. Following the huge success of Dev Patel (who played Anwar), Ron's mother insisted he audition as she has a firm belief that he will be the next 'Slumdog Millionaire'. At 22, Ron is one of the oldest members of the cast and is keeping up his studies while he filming the show. Majoring in Political Science at the University of Toronto, Ron is keen to continue acting after his studies and says he wants to be 'free from judgement' in life.

SOFIA BLACK-D'ELIA

Sofia plays Tea, an open and proud lesbian. Her character is based on Maxxie from the very first UK line-up, and the producers originally had the part down as a gay male called

Theo. They changed their minds at the eleventh hour and quickly had to cast a girl. This is not Sofia's first TV appearance – she played Bailey, a pregnant teenager, in the US hit soap *All My Children*.

Sofia, 18, first auditioned for the character of Michelle and was disappointed when she was not successful. But she soon found out she would be playing Tea and went shopping with her mother to celebrate before going out to get spectacularly drunk. Sounds like she has the *Skins* spirit.

V is for...

Virginity

Virginity (and the loss of it) is a recurring theme in *Skins*. Once, in the not-too-distant past, boys did their best to lose theirs as soon as they could, and 'nice' girls did their best to hold onto their own, at least until Mr Right came along. Now, the girls are right up there with the boys in their eagerness to get deflowered, at least according to *Skins*. Sid is considered a total loser by Tony because he has not lost his cherry, Anwar has to wait until he gets to Russia on the school trip before he gets his oats, and JJ gets his induction from his friend, the lesbian Emily, who does it as a 'once in a lifetime charity event'. This drew criticism from some quarters of the lesbian community, who thought it created classic and highly offensive stereotyping and undermined what it means to be a lesbian. Pandora is desperate for a bit of 'surf and turf', and Mini is so ashamed of being still unravished that she keeps it a secret.

Vomiting

The characters in *Skins* do a lot of throwing up. Hardly an episode goes by without boys or girls demonstrating the excesses of reckless drinking by heaving onto dance floors, pavements and alleyways. There are also many convincing displays of projectile vomiting. But the star prize must go to Mini, who throws up in a boy's lap as she is about to demonstrate her skill at oral sex.

W is for...

Will Merrick (plays Alo Creevy)

Absolute beginner Will Merrick is another example of the way *Skins* has brought a new generation of acting talent to our screens. He says of himself, 'I play the guitar but I'm a bit of a dosser really. I like the Hitchcock films, *Psycho,* and *The Birds.* I am a massive fan of Ralph Fiennes. The English Patient is one of my favourite films of all times. *Reservoir Dogs* too, Tarantino is a bit of a legend. In music, I love The Walkmen, The Stokes, Radiohead, Bombay Bicycle Club, The National, The XX, and The Yeah Yeah Yeahs are one of my favourite bands, they are awesome!' Merrick plays the role of Alo – short for Aloysius – a West Country farm boy now at college in the big city of Bristol (though he still goes home to the farm every night). Alo likes spliff, masturbation, and his dog, Rags.

He's a big-hearted, cheerfully friendly joker who wants to find all the drugs, adventures and good times Bristol can offer. An uncomplicated character, Alo easily manages to find the drugs and the good times, but he's not so successful in his hunt for girls. With very basic interests, he's a very positive sort of guy. No task is too hard, and everything is an adventure.

When interviewed by Channel 4 Will Merrick said of his character:

> I love his sense of humour. I think most of what Alo says and the humour of Alo just comes out of the way he is. He's not really trying to be funny. He's great fun to play, he's got a lot of interaction with a lot of other characters, and he's just a really upbeat kind of guy and so is a very happy part to play. He brings everything really down to earth because things can get quite heated and quite intense within the group and there are lots of fights, arguments, and feuds between the characters and I think Alo really brings everyone together because he is very neutral. Nothing is ever that bad to Alo, so he puts a smile on people's faces.

Asked if he would have liked to play any of the other characters in the series, Will says:

> Nick. At first he's the perfect golden boy and he has everything going for him. Nick has a massive fall, which I think would have been great to do. I'd also love to play Matty because he is so mysterious and no one really knows what is going on with him. I'd quite like to play Mini as well, just be a bit of a bitch. Alo is so nice and doesn't ever upset anyone.

Will Young (plays T. Love)

Making a hilarious cameo appearance in series four, Will plays T. Love, the student advice counsellor, employed to help the Roundview students with any personal or academic worries they may have.

T. Love, an eccentric and useless counsellor with a strange obsession with Michael Jackson, attempts to counsel Freddie when his college work suffers as a result of his destructive love for Effy. In a hilarious exchange between T. and Freddie, T. asks Freddie what Michael Jackson would say if he knew how Freddie's grades were suffering. Amusingly, Freddie replies (in reference to the Jackson songs), 'I'm Bad. Beat It.' T. counters, 'No, he would say "Want to be Startin Something".'

OPPOSITE: SINGER WILL YOUNG BRANCHED OUT INTO ACTING AND PLAYS THE CONVINCING STUDENT ADVICE COUNSELLOR.

Will, who has sold more than eight million records, first caught the public attention when he won *Pop Idol* in 2002. His debut single *Evergreen*, which was released in March 2002, became the fastest-selling debut in UK chart history, selling 403, 027 copies on its day of release. Since then he has gone on to record four platinum and multi-award winning albums.

Will expanded his career into acting in 2005 when he appeared with Dame Judi Dench in the movie *Mrs Henderson Presents* and followed this with a variety of film and TV roles. He is currently starring in Sky TV's supernatural thriller *Bedlam* along with *Skins* co-stars Lily Loveless and Hugo Speer.

Will, who only appeared twice in one episode of *Skins*, said that filming the show made him feel young and beautiful still, like the rest of the cast.

Writers

Skins was created by father-and-son team Bryan Elsey and Jamie Brittain. Elsey was already a highly successful writer and had a string of hit series to his credit, including *Nature Boy*, *The Young Person's Guide to Becoming a Rock Star* and *Rose and Maloney*. When Elsey had the idea to write a teenage drama, his son Jamie, who was then only 21, urged him to reach out beyond the usual teenage clichés and produce something with real relevance to young people's lives. Although he put it rather more bluntly than that. According to

SkinsOnline.com, Elsey revealed that when he ran some of his ideas by Jamie, Jamie said, 'That's a load of old bollocks, Dad.' So Elsey, thinking he was being a smartarse, said, 'What would you do?'

Jamie had a ready answer: 'Get rid of the moralising, the constant pumping rock music that old people seem to think kids like, the middle-aged portrayal of emotions, the issue-based stories, the crap voiceovers and the glammed up 20-something actors who play them. Get rid of all that shite and do something *funny* instead.'

Elsey took the idea to Company pictures who offered it to E4.

'They almost bit our hands off,' recalls Elsey. 'It was the fastest commission I ever got.' *Skins* was born then and there.

The creators also felt that they needed a group of young writers to bring the show to life and it is a tradition of the show to bring in inexperienced writers who can bring fresh ideas with them to grow with the group.

'We generally employ playwrights as writers,' Jamie revealed to PressPlus1.com. 'They tend to be emerging talents, having had one or two professional productions of their stuff that have proved popular. That method means we often find ourselves with young writers who have never written for television before but are not jaded by years of working in what can often be a thankless industry. After a couple of years they are pretty well trained and have written some of our very best episodes.'

Always on the lookout for fresh talent, the creators have

also held competitions for members of the public to win the chance to write for the show.

'In terms of how we work, we all just sit in a big room a couple of times a week and argue for a few hours,' laughs Jamie. 'It takes a long time but we generally come up with goods.

'Each writer in charge of an episode is pretty much allowed to write what they want so that means the tone can swing quite violently between episodes. But I think that is a good thing, the public never know what they are getting with an episode of *Skins*.'

Over the years there have been some big differences of opinion on what should go in to the script. Sometimes Jamie has felt some storylines worked better on paper than on screen. He told PressPlus1.com, 'The Mad Twatter character wasn't as good as it could have been. It wasn't a disaster or anything, but we are much better now and the show was just taking shape then.

'I was absolutely dead set against the singing at the end of series one though. But then I saw it and it was so sweet, refreshing and original and I was brought round. It seemed like such a risk to me, but it worked and I am happy to say I was proved wrong.'

Elsey, who left the show at the end of series four, told SkinsOnline.com, 'I've tried to think about what makes *Skins* different. I think it's that *Skins* reflects the nuances of teenager's lives which are as complex and as emotionally rich as any adults. We are so busy telling teenagers how to behave that we miss the whole picture. We are obsessed with drugs, with drinking, with sex. Young people accept these things as givens. Lecturing them is hopeless. Understanding them is impossible. You can only watch and wander at how well the vast majority of them survive. That's what *Skins* is about. Oh, and it's funny too.'

X,Y AND Z is for...

X-rated

Episodes of *Skins* must be broadcast after the watershed time of 9.00 p.m. because – though the show is about teenagers – the themes are adult (often in the extreme). No punches are pulled when dealing with sex, homosexuality, abortion, drug taking, and violence. Language is raw and some critics consider the attitude of many characters to be repellent. The shows were given an 18 certificate for release on DVD, ironically making them out of bounds for most of the teenagers who form the fan base.

YouTube

The internet has played a massive role in keeping fans abreast of storylines and *Skins* news, and YouTube has been instrumental in this.

Put 'Skins TV' into YouTube and it returns a colossal 5000 pages. Thousands of clips showing fans' favourite episodes, seminal plots and interviews with the cast can be viewed with the opportunity to post comments.

The US version is catching up fast, with over 2000 pages dedicated to the new adaptation.

Youth Culture

Despite the frequent images of wild sex and drug taking synonymous with today's youth, *Skins* also depicts many other examples of youth culture.

Whereas culture itself is defined as being a set of ways a group behaves or a sharing of beliefs, the term 'youth culture' tends to relate to processes and symbolic systems that young people share which are, to some degree, distinctive and separate from those of their parents and the other adults in their community.

Examples in *Skins* include:

Revealing clothing, skateboarding, wacky hairstyles, graffiti, music, alienation from parents, student politics, teen language, hang outs (such as Freddie's shed), peer pressure, cheating on exams. And then of course, like many generations before them, the youth just cannot get enough of 'sex, drugs and rock n roll'.

Zeitgeist

It is true to say that, unlike any TV show aimed at teenagers before it, *Skins* captures the zeitgeist of today's very modern youth. When creators Bryan Elsey and Jamie Brittain penned their very first script, their depiction of what it feels like to be a teenager in Britain today truly illustrated the spirit of the times.

Some elements of life are exaggerated for dramatic reasons, but *Skins* draws the attention of millions of fans because it is true to life and not just a sanitised, preachy TV show.

The show has sold and been screened all over the world and is just as popular in South Korea and Brazil as it is in Europe.